Story Keepers

Story Keepers

A
Journey Into
Native American
Spirituality

John James Stewart

PREMIUM PRESS AMERICA
NASHVILLE, TENNESSEE

Story Keepers by John James Stewart
©2001 John James Stewart
Updated Edition ©2016 PREMIUM PRESS AMERICA
Published by PREMIUM PRESS AMERICA

ISBN 978-1-887654-56-2
Library of Congress Catalog Card Number 2002091254

PREMIUM PRESS AMERICA books are available at special discounts for premiums, sales promotions, fundraising, or educational use. For details contact the distributor at 6581 Jocelyn Hollow Road, Nashville TN 37205-3950, phone toll-free 800-891-7323, fax 615-353-7905, or email orders@premiumpressamerica.com

www.premiumpressamerica.com

Cover by John James Stewart
Layout by Booksetters / Booksetters@aol.com

Printed in the United States of America
6 7 8 9 10 / 10 9 8 7 6

These stories and legends have always belonged to the Native People of the Americas. And they always will.

Dedicated to

Wapistan, Ursula, Chante, Stone Woman, Elizabeth, Bob, White Eagle, Murray and all the human "Story Keepers" that shared their knowledge with me.

J.J.S.

Editor's Note: The writer and editors have attempted to present these legends in keeping with the spirit of the oral tradition under which they have been preserved and perpetuated through the generations. In doing so, some honorific titles and other proper nouns may vary slightly in capitalization, based on their usage and context.

Table of Contents

Preface

By John James Stewart

Story Keepers in Native communities were held in high regard. They were and are highly trained individuals, instructed by the Elders in the important task of remembering and telling the history and legends of the Tribe. But, in the past, the Story Keepers did not just remember the traditions of the Clans. They were also entertainers, historians, priests, counselors, psychiatrists, zoologists, astronomers and the ones who understood and taught the meaning and origin of the Ceremonies.

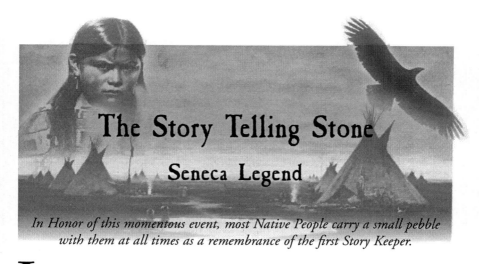

The Story Telling Stone

Seneca Legend

In Honor of this momentous event, most Native People carry a small pebble with them at all times as a remembrance of the first Story Keeper.

Long before the White Men came to the Lands of the Seneca, there lived a boy whose parents had died. He lived with his grandparents. The orphan's grandparents were very good to him and taught him well. Not just about hunting and gathering food, but about Spiritual things and the meaning of the Ceremonies. He grew strong and brave, but most of all—he grew wise.

One day his grandfather handed him a grown man's hunting bow and told him that they would go on a hunt together. It was the boy's first real hunt and he was very excited. In the woods nearby, his grandfather showed him how to use the bow in a proper manner. He also explained why he should never kill more of Creator's creatures than the People could use. He was also taught to Pray for the Souls of the animals and birds that would give themselves to him.

Soon after that, the boy went hunting on his own, and he quickly became very good at it. He not only supplied his own family with food, but he took care of a lot of others, including People who had no one to hunt for them. Many families came to rely on him.

One day, when the boy was deep in the forest, Father Sun began to slip down the Sky. The boy was hungry so he sat on a large Rock to eat a little of the parched corn his grandmother had given him. He put down his pack, with the game inside, beside the Rock and started to eat. A strange voice said, "Would you like to hear a story?" The voice seemed to come from nowhere.

"Who said that?" demanded the boy, jumping up and looking around apprehensively.

"The Stone on which you now stand speaks to you," came the eerie reply. Stone's voice then continued, "Would you like to hear a story?"

The boy was a little shaken but remembered what his grandfather had told him—everything can communicate with us, usually we choose not to listen.

"Yes, I would like to hear a story," said the boy, still feeling very uneasy.

"Then, you must give me something, an offering, give me the game that you have killed, and I will tell you many stories, stories that will be of great importance to you and your People."

The boy did as he was asked, taking the game from the bag and placing it on the large Rock. Stone began to tell stories. The boy listened to the fascinating tales, until Sun was almost gone, His soft light peering from just

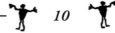

10

above the Western horizon, barely managing to penetrate the thick, forest foliage. Stone had told him many, wonderful legends.

"I must go, Stone," said the boy. "It will be dark before I reach my village, and my grandparents will be worried. I will return tomorrow."

After bidding farewell to Stone, he hurried back to his village. On the way home, he managed to bag a Rabbit and two small birds just before Father Sun's light faded altogether.

When he reached the village, he saw his grandparents standing in the poor light afforded by a cloud-shrouded Moon. They looked worried. When they saw their grandson, their faces lit up with loving smiles. His grandfather put his arm around the boy's shoulders, and they walked back to their lodge.

"It seems you did not fare well today in the hunt," said his grandmother, looking into her grandson's pack.

The boy, not wishing to sound foolish by telling his grandparents about the Talking Stone, lied to his grandmother. "I think I have over hunted the woods that are close to our camp. I will have to go deeper tomorrow."

His grandfather spoke up, saying, "A lot of People have come to rely on you, but you can only kill the animals that will give their lives to you. No more."

Early the next day, the boy set out again. He killed some small game, then made his way as quickly as he could to the Story Telling Stone. When he reached

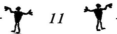

the place where Stone lay, he made the offering of the game he had killed, saying, "Stone, here is what I offer you. Please tell me more stories."

Stone did and the boy listened all day to the wonderful stories about the beginning of Earth Mother and how animals were named. He heard many, many great stories. Again, Sun had almost left the Sky before he started for home. This time, all he killed on the way home was a very small bird just before Sky turned black. Luckily for the boy, Sister Moon was now full and She shone brightly and lit his trail well with Her silvery light. When he reached the edge of the village, there stood his worried-looking grandparents once more.

After they returned to the Lodge, he gave his grandparents the small bird. His grandfather said, "We will go hungry tonight, my grandson. Have you lost your hunting skills? Other boys and men were hunting today in the same forest and brought much game home. They have given plenty to the needy. So, at least they will not go hungry."

Again the boy lied, "Grandfather, I must have been unlucky. That's all. I will do better tomorrow."

"Don't worry," interrupted his grandmother. "We will not really go hungry tonight. I have lots of corn. I will make hominy for us, and we will eat it with the meat from this little bird. After that is gone, I have berries that I picked today. We will eat well."

The next morning, the boy set out early, determined to do a better job of hunting. He walked stealthily through the woods, stalking and gathering

12

many animals and birds. It was as his grandfather had said. They gave their lives to him, so he could feed his family. Soon, he was close to the clearing where Stone lived.

"Have you come to hear more legends?" Stone called out to him.

"Stone," he said, "I would love to hear more stories, but I have to hunt for my family and for the needy of our village. Alas, Your Wisdom will not fill their bellies. I cannot afford to give you any more game."

"Sit, Orphan, and listen," said the Stone. "Because of your generosity, I will share all My knowledge with you and your People. Tomorrow, gather the Tribe and bring them to Me. You have given Me a lot, in fact, all you had in your game bag. I will give your People, in return, everything I know. Tell the People to bring enough food for four days."

The boy went back to his village before dark and gave his full game bag to his proud grandparents. He then set off to talk to the Leader of the village. He told Her what had happened, and the Leader called a Council of the Elders who agreed to go and see this strange Story Telling Stone.

The next morning, the whole village set off with the boy in the lead. Soon, they came to the clearing where Stone lived. The boy bade them sit, to be quiet and humble, in the presence of such a Great Story Teller.

"Stone, I have done as You asked. Our People are all here."

"Very well," said Stone. Then, in a louder voice he said, "All of you listen carefully to what I am about to tell you. I, Stone, and my Brothers and

Sisters were the first things created here on Earth. We have been here since the very beginning. Therefore, We know everything, the complete History of Earth Mother. I am going to tell stories of great importance. These are the legends which tell how the People came to be. They tell of Creation, the battles that cleared Earth Mother of the Evil Monsters, so that the People may come and live in peace.

"These stories must be kept and handed down from generation to generation. You must assign People with good memory as Story Keepers, so that they can pass these legends on," said Stone. "These stories contain the Wisdom, the Knowledge and Insight the People will need to get through the turmoil to come. These are the stories that will tell the Seneca of their history."

Why Bear Waddles

Comanche Legend

If you have seen Bear, upright or on all fours, you may have noticed that he waddles when he walks. The reason why may surprise you.

Along, long time ago, before the Human People came, Sun and Moon held on to their power as long as they possibly could, causing days and nights to be much longer than they are now.

The Night People such as Bat, Mole, Owl and Coyote liked Night, and wanted it all the time. The Day People such as Buffalo, Deer, Rabbit, Elk and Prairie Chicken wanted Sun to shine all the time. In those days, the animals and birds were always squabbling about Night and Day; they had come close to having a war over it.

It was decided a Grand Council would be held and it would be held at night with Moon and Sun in attendance. Sun said He would not come if Moon was there, and He didn't.

However, the animals and birds did meet to try and sort out their differences. Those who wanted Sun to govern gathered together to talk to those who wanted Moon to rule. Everyone started bickering.

"This will not do. We must have order," shouted Buffalo. "Each side pick someone who will speak for all." Everyone calmed down a little and got on with picking their speakers. The Night People chose Coyote and the Sun People chose Buffalo. They met and talked but neither side could agree.

Bear, who was sitting with the Night People, spoke up saying, "Why don't we play a game of chance, a contest? We will have Moon People play against the Sun People. The winner will decide what is to be done." Everyone thought that it was a splendid idea. So a game of Hide the Bones started. The Sun side had the Bones first and were very skillful at passing them from one paw or claw to another. They were soon in the lead. But then, Mole got really lucky and the Moon People caught up. The game had gone on for so long that Bear, who at best was always a very sleepy fellow, got tired. He took his moccasins off and lay down to rest. He was soon fast asleep.

All this time, Sun was waiting under Earth to find out His fate. But the game went on and on with first one side winning and then the other. Sun could not wait for what He considered a bunch of silly animals and birds to end their feud, so He started His climb into the Sky, bathing everything in His path with warm, orange light as He lifted Himself into the Eastern Sky.

16

The Night People hated Sun. When they saw Him coming, they were very upset, thinking Sun had taken power before the outcome of the Game being played had come to a conclusion. And, of course, Moon was extremely disturbed with the uncalled for presence of Sun. The game was still a tie. Soon, the light became so intense that all the Night People had to hide. Bear got up to leave and, in his hurry to get away, he put his moccasins on the wrong feet. He didn't want to be around when Sun turned into a ball of fire high in the Sky, so he tried to run with his moccasins pinching his feet; the pain made him waddle from side to side.

Sun shouted to Moon, "We cannot leave Our destinies to these quarrelsome creatures. You and I should decide a matter as important as this."

So Sun and Moon had a meeting, talked over what had happened and how They could better share Their power. After a lot of arguing, They came to a decision. Father Sun said, "I will go first and I will rise in the East. When I reach the West, it will be Your turn to rule until I rise again. In that way, it will be fair to the Moon and Sun Peoples and to Us, as well."

And so it was that what we have come to consider normal days and nights came about. But Moon still cheats a little, especially in the Summertime. If you look up into the morning or late evening Skies, you will often see Moon hanging on to Her power for as long as She possibly can.

To this day Bear wears his moccasins on the wrong feet and still waddles.

Buffalo Mountain

Kiowa Legend

The annihilation of the Buffalo, along with the many diseases which the White Man brought to Native Peoples, led to the demise of many Tribes. Some Native People still believe Buffalo are waiting under the ground for a time when they can re-emerge.

There was a time, not that long ago, when the Buffalo were so plentiful that some areas of the plains appeared black with them. A hunter could ride for days along the perimeter of one herd.

In those days, the Plains Tribes revered the animal. It had become almost a god to them, a Life-Giver. They used everything from the beast. The meat was used for food; the hide for clothes, blankets and coverings for their teepees; the sinew for bow strings and ties; the bladders as water containers; the hooves for glue; and the bones for ladles, pins and needles. The toughest part of the hide, the neck, was used to make the small, round war-shields which plains warriors carried. Buffalo wool was gathered and used as stuffing for pillows. Even Buffalo excrement was used as fuel for fires.

Following a Buffalo hunt, the best hide was kept as an offering. Painted by the finest artist to commemorate the event, it was returned to the site where the hunt had taken place and left at the highest point to Honor the Buffalo that had given their lives so the People could live. This show of respect was also meant to Honor the Souls of the Buffalo and their passing from Earth to the Spirit World. Plains Tribes believed if the Buffalo were hunted in a Sacred Manner, they would return to be hunted again. In this way, the Circle of Life and Death would last forever.

The skulls of the Buffalo were also considered Holy and used in the Sacred Sun Dance Ceremony. Skulls left on the prairie were always turned to the East, facing where Father Sun rises. Native North Americans lived as one with their Life-Giver, the Buffalo.

When the White Men first came to the Plains, it seemed to the Native People that they just wanted to trade. Soon, however, the Whites began to covet the lands where the First Nations People lived. They tried to take the land from them by force but the Natives fought back and fought hard. In retaliation, the White Government sent its Army to kill the Native People's food supply—Buffalo.

During this time, a young Kiowa warrior and his family had been running from the White Soldiers. They were camped in a valley near

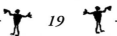

Beautiful Mountain in very rugged terrain which they hoped would deter the soldiers from following them.

One morning, the young warrior's wife had risen early. She had gone to draw water from a stream when she heard the sound of hooves clattering on the stony ground. Afraid that her warrior husband's assumptions about the White Soldiers not being able to follow them were wrong, she hid in the thick undergrowth, fearing for her life, expecting the worse.

It had been quite cold the night before and the warmth of the morning Sun had caused a thick mist to form, carpeting the valley floor. Through the mist emerged a huge, white, female Buffalo, leading some badly scarred, young Buffalo warriors, their wives and children. The small Buffalo party stopped and looked sadly at the young woman in her hiding place, as if to say, "Good-bye." Then they lumbered on to the foot of Beautiful Mountain. When they got to its base, the side of the mountain opened. The interior was a Magical Place where Sun always shone and the waters were clear and cool, where the birds sang and the grass was the greenest green. Irreverent hunters were non-existent and respect for everything was the only Way of Life.

The White Buffalo Woman led the party inside and Beautiful Mountain closed behind them. The White Man had won. The Buffalo were gone.

 20

Coyote-Eagle

Yakima Legend

Failing to appreciate and respect special skills can lead to disappointment, even for Trickster, Coyote.

I t was a beautiful, warm, sunny day with a brisk wind that kept the temperature from getting too high. Wind blew through Coyote's fur as He stood stiff-legged, head held high, eyes tightly closed, savoring the feeling. Coyote opened His eyes and saw Eagle soaring high in the Sky, swooping, dipping and diving. "I wish I could fly," He said to Himself. "I love the way the wind caresses My body and flying looks like such fun. Imagine all the Squirrels I could get if only I could fly." Coyote started to drool at the very thought of such tasty, fuzzy little morsels.

It is well known by all that Eagle has great sight. What is not so well understood is that He also has very keen hearing. Even from such a great height, He heard Coyote mumbling to Himself and swooped lower to investigate.

"So, Coyote wishes to fly," said Eagle to the surprised Coyote.

"Yes. I would very much like to fly," replied Coyote.

"Then You shall. Climb to the bluff above Us," said Eagle, indicating a high, overhanging cliff above them.

Feeling very apprehensive about the whole thing, Coyote did as He was bid. He then sat nervously peeking over the edge of the bluff, looking at the valley floor far below.

Eagle landed close by and in a serious tone of voice said, "During the Ceremony that will make You able to fly, I will pass over You five times. You must count them. I will then pass over You for the fifth and last time and I will touch You with My wings. You will then be ready to fly. As I pass over the last time, You must jump from the bluff into the Sky. I will do the rest. Are You ready?"

"As ready as I will ever be," said Coyote, trying His best to be brave. "You aren't trying to trick Me, are You, Eagle?"

Eagle replied in a stern tone, "I am Eagle. I do as I say I will. I play no tricks. I leave that domain to You."

Eagle began His passes, swooping low and very close to the terrified Coyote. On the fourth pass Eagle flew so close to Coyote that our canine friend could feel the air being pushed from Eagle's powerful wing strokes.

"Be ready, Coyote. Be ready to jump," warned Eagle as He got prepared to make His final pass. Eagle flew up to Coyote, touching Him as He said He would.

22

Coyote jumped, but not into the Sky as Eagle had commanded. Instead, He leapt back from the precipice.

"What's this? Brave Coyote, Our famous Trickster is frightened of flying!" scoffed Eagle.

"No, Eagle. I'm frightened of falling to My death," said Coyote in a very matter-of-fact tone.

"I would not allow You to fall, My Friend. I will give You one more chance, Coyote. If You do not wish to fly, I will leave You. I have better things to do with My time," said Eagle disdainfully.

So, still wishing to have the power of flight, Coyote nervously approached and sat on the edge of the high bluff, not daring to look down. This time, on Eagle's fifth pass, Eagle again touched Coyote lightly with His wing. Coyote jumped out into space, leaving the cliff edge behind Him. Down, down, down He went, flying about as well as Rock can.

"You lying Son of a....," screamed Coyote.

"Open Your front legs, Coyote, not Your silly mouth!" Eagle shouted to the plummeting Coyote. "Your front legs have become wings."

Sure enough, it was true. Coyote opened His front legs and immediately and for the very first time, found Himself flying. It wasn't long before He had the new experience mastered. It only took a very short time before He was swooping through the Sky, diving and climbing, doing all sorts of daring aerobatics with great dexterity. He had become Coyote-Eagle.

Then, far below, came the moment Coyote-Eagle had most wanted. He spied Squirrel perched in a tree. "Ha," He thought. "Here is my chance to have a nice lunch." He plunged down towards the unsuspecting rodent and was soon sitting on the bluff He had started out from, munching on His quarry. Of course, Coyote, being a greedy sort of fellow, was soon off again hunting for more unsuspecting Squirrel and found many.

Eagle had stayed close by and had been watching greedy Coyote. He commented, "If You eat too many Squirrel, Coyote, You will become too fat to fly."

Coyote didn't care. He jumped into the Sky, looking for more food.

Another Coyote, a very pretty female, saw Coyote-Eagle floating and flapping around in the clear blue Sky and wished to have the same power. Especially so when she saw Him swooping down on her all-time favorite meal—Squirrel. She shouted up to Coyote-Eagle, calling upon Him to give her the power of flight.

Of course, Coyote, being a conceited fellow, thought He now owned the secret of flight and agreed to show the pretty, young girl Coyote His Secret. He got her to perch on the bluff where He had first sat. He then swooped as low and as close as He could to her. On the fifth pass He touched her lightly with His wings. She jumped backwards, just as Coyote-Eagle had the first time, fearing for her life.

24

"Don't be afraid. You must trust Me," shouted Coyote-Eagle. "This time, when I touch You with My wings You must jump from the ledge. Your front legs will turn into wings and you will be able to fly, just like Me."

And so it was the girl Coyote plucked up enough courage to do as she was bid. This time, when Coyote-Eagle brushed past her, she jumped into space just as Coyote-Eagle had demanded. However, her legs did not turn into wings and she plunged to the valley floor below. Coyote-Eagle was unable to help her. Luckily, some dense bushes broke her fall and she was not killed, although very badly shaken. Not surprisingly, she had some rather harsh words for Coyote-Eagle, some of them were the kind lady Coyotes hardly ever use.

With the screeching sound that only Eagle can make, He swooped out of the Sky and landed by the canine pair, "You do not have My power, Coyote. Creator gave Me the power to make others fly. He also gave Me the power to take that gift away if it was misused. If You had My power, there would be too many Coyote-Eagles in the Sky. And with Your appetites, I would have nothing to eat Myself. So, I think it only fitting that I take Your power of flight away."

And so, because of His conceit and the danger He had put the lady Coyote in, Coyote-Eagle's flying skills were taken from Him. Left without the ability to fly, He sat next to the pretty, female Coyote on the wind-swept valley floor. So, there they were, two Coyotes staring at one another. Coyote grinned. Girl Coyote fluttered her eye lashes and looked away coyly.

I am told that after they got over the fact that they would not be able to fly and the scolding she had given Coyote wore off, they became good friends—very good friends. Some say, they even made more Coyotes.

Death

Blackfoot Legend

Each creature lives a life span as deemed appropriate by Creator. Along the way, Creator creates Unexpected Death and learns even He must live with the consequences.

Creator, who had already made Mother Earth, Sky, Water and the animals, birds, fish and vegetation that lived on Her, came to a very important decision. He had always thought that one more animal was needed—an animal that could care for and help to maintain His Earth, one with more intelligence than the other creatures. He wasn't quite sure what this new animal should look like or feed upon but He had decided to call His new creations People.

Creator went for a long walk to mull over the many possibilities for shape, size and expertise of the new creatures. He could come to no special conclusions. So, He went to His Wife to ask for help in developing this new specimen. He found Her sewing beads onto a new pair of moccasins that She had just made for Him.

"You do truly beautiful work, My Wife," said Creator, picking up one of the moccasins and admiring it. "I am going to make what may well be My finest creation. I will call them People. I am going to put them on Earth to live among the other things I have already made. But I have to be very careful for I'm going to give these creatures more intelligence than any that I have created so far.

"I have thought this matter over carefully, but I do not have all the answers, so, please, can You help?" Creator asked. His Wife nodded acceptance with a smile and He continued.

"This animal, when produced, will be mentally and physically capable of ruining everything I have created on Earth," Creator said. "So, We will have to be extremely careful with its development. As You well know, once We have come to Our decisions on its conception, We cannot go back on them. For the sake of order, when Our conclusions are reached, We must abide by them. They must remain final. It is of the utmost importance We get everything right or I may have to use My power of destruction and exterminate them all at a later date."

"Well, You do sound very serious," She smiled. "Of course, I would be happy to help in any way I can. What will these People look like, Husband?" She asked, trying to lighten the conversation a little. "Not like ugly Spider, I hope," She gave a little shudder.

"I like Spider. He's a cute, fuzzy little fellow. But, no, I think I will make these People look like Bear but maybe not so hairy. I like Bear. He's big and strong."

"Yes, that would be good, sort of like Bear. But I think it would be more fitting if they looked a bit more like You, Husband. Why don't You make them in Your own image?" Then smiling, she added as an afterthought. "With, of course, some small differences. Perhaps not quite so serious," She giggled.

Creator did not appear to catch this minor humorous, admonishment and carried on, "You think so, My Dear, like Me, eh?" Creator pondered for a moment, weighing Her suggestion carefully, then smiling, His mind made up. "Good, then I will make them look like Me but without My powers. That would be too much for them to cope with! So, that's decided. Oh, and perhaps I will make them a little more light-hearted than I am," He grinned, knowingly.

His wife smiled and asked, "What will they eat?"

"To stop any population explosions among My creatures, I think they should eat the flesh of the animals and birds that I have already created. I will give the People a special call, and when they use it, the animals and birds will come. They can kill what they need to survive."

Creator's Wife responded, "Well that's not a bad idea, but You know, if You make it too easy for them to obtain meat, they may become lazy. Why don't

29

You make them hunt and track their quarry in the same way the animals and birds do? They should have to discipline themselves to think as the animals and birds do in the way of the hunt. That way, they will become strong and wise from searching for their food. In turn, the animals, too, will become stronger and wiser because of the pursuit. It should keep a good balance."

"You are very wise, My Wife. It will be done the way You say." As an afterthought, He added, "I think before they hunt, they should Pray to the creatures that are to give their flesh so that the creature's Spirit may endure. It is fitting that they should Pray for the safekeeping of the creature's Spirits. I will not make it too easy for the People. I will make some of My animals stronger than they are now, so that they can hunt for the People's flesh—perhaps Bear, Wolf and Cat."

"That is good, Husband. Also, apart from eating the flesh of the animals and birds, I think Your new People should also be able to consume plants and fish. That way, most of the things You have created will become a food resource to them," added His Wife.

"Then, that, too, is decided and so it shall be," He said.

And so Creator created People in His own image, and the People flourished. Soon, there were many of them—too many. They had eaten most of the game; all their natural food resources were now in short supply.

Creator said to His Wife, "I think I will have to destroy these People. Things are not going nearly as well as I thought they would. The People have become the dominant creature on Earth. They have become so good at hunting, that they have killed off many of My animals, some species to near extinction. Even the animals I made predators of People have become frightened of them. I thought they would learn to conserve, not waste!"

"You need not exterminate them. I think what You should do is give everything You have created a length of time on Earth, a Life Span of whatever time You feel is correct," said His Wife.

"You know I cannot alter what I have already created," He said.

"But You have not created Life Spans, yet," She argued.

"I think I know what You mean," said Creator, pausing to contemplate. He continued, "Everything will only be allowed to exist for a period of time. All life forms will have an allotted term of existence. What shall We call this thing that ends this Life Span?" asked Creator.

"The condition of the creature that falls prey to another, after there has been a successful hunt, is now called Death. It will be the state when a creature's life is relinquished for another's sake. So, let the end of any life be called Death."

"So it will be. I will give all the things that I have created a Life Span." He said, pausing again to formulate a new idea. "At this time, I also will make strange maladies that will occur for no apparent reason and which My creatures will not understand and call it Sudden Death. Hopefully, this will

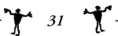

cull the weak and infirm from among My conceptions. This Death will affect all things except Rock.

"Rock is part of My body and will not be part of this newly-made Life Span," said Creator, solemnly.

"My Husband, if You are making this rule for all, then You must give Rock a Life Span, too, even though it is part of Your body. It would be unfair to set Rock apart from Your other Creations."

Creator contemplated Her demand, "You are correct, as always. I will give Rock the longest of all the Life Spans. However, it, too, eventually will crumble and die."

So it was that unexpected and anticipated Death came to be.

At about this time, Creator and His Wife were expecting Their first baby and had been looking forward to the event with great anticipation. Unfortunately, the child, a female, was born prematurely and just after her birth, the tiny girl, took sick and died.

Creator's Wife came crying to Him, begging Him too change the newly created rules of Death. She implored Him to alter the rules for the sake of Their baby.

"No, My Wife," He shook His head sadly. "We cannot make rules for Our Creations that We are not willing to keep Ourselves. All Our decisions must remain final. We alone make the rules. We cannot break them."

Creator sat considering His painful decision with the tears of sorrow for His little child's death in His eyes. He then added, "But, I will create a Spirit World, a World where the Souls of the Dead may go. It will be a place where Our little daughter's Spirit and all the departed Souls can be happy, forever."

Spider Brings Fire

Cherokee Legend

Size doesn't matter.

A long, long time ago, before the Two Leggeds (men), the People who lived on Mother Earth were Wing Flappers (birds), Four Leggeds (animals), Little People of the Air and Earth (insects) and Slitherers (reptiles). None of these Peoples owned the gift of fire. Only the Thunder Beings owned the secret of fire. Sometimes, they sent an emissary (Lightning) to set fire on the land, but the creatures did not know how to catch it.

One day the Thunder Beings sent Lightning to Mother Earth. It hit an old tree on an island near a village where Wing Flappers lived.

The Leader of the People saw the old tree on fire and immediately held Council.

"This may be our opportunity to catch fire. If we had it, we would be warm in Winter. Whoever goes must do it by swimming or flying across to the island, for that is where the Thunderbirds have placed fire, in an old tree there. Who will volunteer to fetch it?"

"I will," said Crow, who at that time was a beautiful bird with snow white plumage and a wonderful singing voice.

"Very well, Crow, good luck, Creator be with you. Let us all hope you succeed in your mission," said the Leader.

Crow flew out to the island and landed on a branch of the old tree. Just then, the wind came up and caused a huge cloud of billowing smoke to envelope Crow. Coughing and sputtering, Crow flew home, unable to complete his task. From that day on Crow has kept the smoke-blackened feathers and dry, raspy throat received when he tried to gain fire for his People. The gift for his bravery was that he become one of Mother Nature's most dowdy birds; he definitely has one of the worst singing voices.

Next, Screech Owl said he would try, and he flapped out to the island and landed on a branch close to the flames. Again, the wind fanned the flames and they engulfed Screech Owl, singeing his face. Ever since then, Screech Owl has had sore, red eyes, and it hurts him to blink, that is why he hardly ever does and by the way his singing voice is not much better than Crow's.

It was decided to ask some of the other People to help and they sent for the Slitherers and the Little People of the Air and Earth.

The next to try was Bigsnake, who at that time had beautiful pink skin. He swam quickly out to the island and slithered, stealthily, up to the burning tree. He was just about to grab a burning twig when a smoldering branch fell on him, scorching him badly. From that day to this, he has been known as Blacksnake.

Another Owl said she would go, Great Horned Owl, but she fared no better that the others, and from that day to this has had big rings around her eyes and looks as though she lacks sleep.

The Peoples were about to give up when Water Spider stepped forward.

"I will bring Fire," she said in a very determined manner. The other People laughed.

"You are too small; how could you bring Fire?" They chided.

"It is not the amount of fire that matters. A spark is all we need. As I stated, I will bring Fire, and I will. My sister brought light to these Lands, now I will bring Fire," she replied tersely.

The Leader told all the gathered that it was Spider's right to try, and He wished her well.

Water Spider spun a web and made it into a little bowl. She placed the bowl on her back. Then she set off toward the island, scampering over the top of the water as Water Spiders can. When she reached the island, she waited for an opportunity to catch some Fire without the Fire catching her. When the right time came, she placed one small coal in the bowl she had made and scooted back across the water to her friends on the shore of the lake. And so it was that the Peoples of the Old World gained Fire, and, for a while, were warm in the Winter. But, alas, one bad thunderstorm with its deluge of rain extinguished their Fire. As we all know, at this time they still have not gained it back.

Chakabish and the Geese

Cree Legend

Ever notice a flock of Geese flying overhead in a perfect "V"? Chakabish unintentionally helped them learn to fly that way.

Chakabish, although much younger than Wisakachak, loved to play tricks on animals and birds and in that way was much like the famous Trickster, Wisakachak.

He was hunting during Wey Wey Besum (The Moon of the Snow Goose). As yet, there was no snow on the ground but the nights were getting cold.

"The geese (Wey Wey and Niska) and ducks (Shesheep) will soon fly South for the Winter. It will become more difficult to find enough food," he thought to himself. "I should see if I can catch some before they are all gone."

He came to the edge of a lake where some geese were sitting floating, looking plump and good to eat.

"How can I get out there and catch some?" thought Chakabish. "I know what I'll do." He went into the forest and cut a thin vine. He, then, made his way back to the lake where he silently slipped into the water, swam out beneath the surface and under the geese, pulling his vine and breathing through a hollow reed.

The geese were snoozing and did not notice Chakabish. He took his vine and gently tied their feet together. One of the geese awoke. Realizing something was wrong, it tried to fly off the lake. But Chakabish had snared all of them with his vine.

Chaos reigned. After a lot of splashing about, the head goose shouted, "Our feet have been tied. But if we work as a team, I think we can still escape. I will lead but we must all take off as one."

With the goose Leader in front and the others on either side lined up in a "V" formation, they paddled along as fast as they could go, quickly learning as a team. Once they mastered paddling along together, they slowly lifted from the lake, pulling Chakabish out of the water with them. As they got higher, the vine broke and Chakabish tumbled back into the lake.

This is the reason you always see geese flying in a V formation. They remember what Chakabish did to them. Because they don't want it to happen again, they wisely stick together.

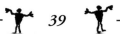

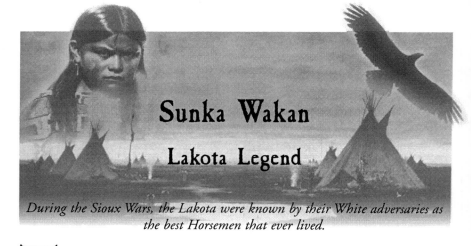

Sunka Wakan

Lakota Legend

During the Sioux Wars, the Lakota were known by their White adversaries as the best Horsemen that ever lived.

There was a time when Dog was the only domesticated animal the Lakota had. They were the pack animals that pulled the travois and Lodges. Some even carried children on their backs. In those days, the Lakota had much smaller teepees because the Dogs were not strong enough to pull the much larger teepees that the Plains Peoples would become famous for later in their history.

The Lakota were a nomadic People who followed the Buffalo. Back then, there were so many Buffalo on the plains that they would often graze right next to the People's encampments, sometimes actually coming into the villages.

One morning, a young warrior got up very early to do a Sunrise Ceremony. It was still dark as he walked into the nearby hills. As he walked, the first hint of gray-blue came into the pre-dawn Sky. Soon, a hint of orange followed and the new light illuminated the prairie in soft, subtle, shades.

As the young man Prayed, he could not help but notice that there were some Buffalo grazing nearby. But what he saw next stopped him Praying, and forced him to react. Among the Buffalo the warrior saw a strange and beautifully graceful beast, one he had never seen before. It was feeding on the prairie grasses. He cautiously walked towards it. On seeing the young man, the Buffalo moved off, but the strange beast did not seem at all afraid. It simply kept on happily cropping the grass. Every now and then, it raised its head to look at the man while still munching away. To the young warrior, the animal seemed like a very large, muscular Dog. "What could it be?" he asked himself.

Suddenly, the animal raised its head, shaking it violently and calling to the warrior in a strange voice. "Whee-nhee-hee," it cried. It appeared to the young man that the animal was talking to him.

The man cautiously watched the strange beast. It had no fear of him. It just stood motionless, occasionally shaking its head and talking to him. On reaching the animal, he patted its neck and spoke softly to it. He then took a rope from his Medicine Bag and gently placed it over the wonderful creature's neck. To his surprise, it did not try to escape. In fact, on giving the rope a slight tug, it meekly followed him to his village. The young warrior called his newfound prize, Sunka Wakan (Holy Dog).

As I have told you, the Dogs sometimes carried children on their backs. The warrior wondered if this Holy Dog, being much larger than its counterparts, would be able to carry him. So, one morning, he plucked up enough courage to get onto the beast's back. Off Sunka Waken charged, with the Warrior clinging to him for dear life, his body bouncing around like a dry leaf, in a fast-running stream. Luckily for the warrior, the animal soon got bored with the game and trotted to a halt, snorting out its acceptance of the man. Within days, the warrior learned to ride the animal well and the two became as one.

Soon, more of these beautiful animals were found on the prairies. From then on, the whole economy of the Lakota as well as many other Plains Peoples was measured by the number Sunka Waken they owned.

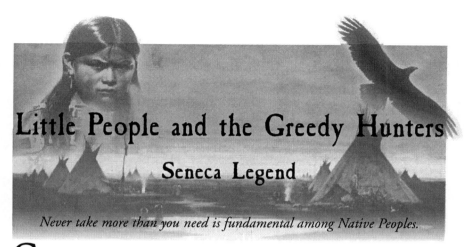

Little People and the Greedy Hunters

Seneca Legend

Never take more than you need is fundamental among Native Peoples.

Some Seneca men were hunting a long way from their main encampment. They found game so plentiful that they killed much more than they needed. Even though their teachings said they should have known better, they had slaughtered so many animals and birds that they could not possibly carry all the butchered meat back to their village, which was a long way away.

There was so much it could not fit onto their sleds. They decided to keep all of the hides and to eat as much of the freshly killed meat as they could. They prepared a big feast and gorged until they could eat no more. The next morning, they packed up the hides, leaving all the uneaten meat in the snow.

"We will feed the Wolves and Ravens as well as we have fed ourselves or better," laughed one of the hunters.

They traveled all day very slowly, the weight of the animal furs and hides causing the sleds to bog down regularly. After a very difficult day, the hunters set up camp again. It was decided that they would have to hunt for food again the next morning, and every morning of the ten Sun's walk from their village.

So the next morning, leaving their precious hides in their makeshift encampment, off they went to hunt for food. They found lots of tracks, and followed them but the tracks disappeared, as if by magic. Search as they may, they couldn't find any game in the new area. They left and headed back to their village. The next morning, they searched for game again and still found none. They were becoming very hungry and it became quite apparent that if they didn't find game soon, they might all starve to death.

That night, Sister Moon shone brightly and one of the hunters took a walk away from the others. He stopped in a clearing, his eyes closed tightly and began Praying to Great Spirit for the gift of food. Then when he felt a tugging at his sleeve. He looked to see who it was, thinking it was one of the other hunters. He was surprised, in fact, shocked to see a Tiny Person standing beside him. He had heard many stories about the Little People and their magical powers, but had never seen one in person. He was very frightened.

"Listen closely to me," said the Little Man. "We Little People have been watching you. We are very annoyed that you hunters have been so wasteful with the flesh of those fine animals and birds that gave themselves to you. We are the reason you can find no game. You are now being punished for your stupidity. You are Praying to Creator for food. I do not think He has ears that will hear you at this time." The hunter now felt great fear.

The Little Man continued, "The Little People have decided that if you wish to live, you must give up all your hides. We will give you until tomorrow to make up your minds. Give up the hides or starve and die." With that said, the Little Person turned and left, disappearing into the forest.

When the hunter who had spoken to the Little People's emissary told the others what he had said, they were all afraid, as they knew in their hearts that they had done wrong. "We cannot give the Little People the hides. Without them, our families will have no new clothes for the Winter," said one of the hunters. They did not know what to do. They were very hungry and knew that without food, they would not make it back to their village, which was still many Suns away. They held Council and came up with a plan.

The next day, the same Little Person who had visited the night before came back. "Well, have you made up your minds as to what you will do?" he asked.

"We have all talked this matter over and realize that we have been very greedy and mindless of our Teachings. To do what we have done to the animals that gave themselves to us is unforgivable. Unfortunately, it cannot be undone and to go back to our People with nothing after such a long hunting trip would be worse than death," said the hunter. "I am afraid we cannot give up all of our hides, as we need them to clothe our families. But we will share with you. You may pick out the best. If we do not make it back to our village, then you may take the rest. We are sorry. Please forgive us for being so disrespectful. We are ready to die, if that is your wish." The hunter hung his head in shame, as did all his friends.

"It is not up to me to forgive you," said the envoy from the Little People. "It is up to our Council of Elders to decide your fate. But I feel you are truly repentant. I will speak to our Elders on your behalf. Now come with me." The Emissary took the hunters to a warm cave. "You must stay here until I return with the verdict of My People. You will be warm here. We have provided enough food to satisfy your hunger."

The hunters thanked the Little Person for His generosity. Apprehensively, they dug into the food that had been supplied, all the while wondering what their fates would be.

The next day, the Little People's envoy arrived with two others from His Tribe. Their smiles heralded the good news. "The Elders have forgiven you, but just this once," said the Spokesman. "Be warned. If this ever happens again, things will not go so well for you. These two Little People have volunteered to guide you to the quickest way back to your village and they will help you to find game on your trek home. Oh, and one other thing. We do not want the hides or furs. You may take them with you for your families. But remember our warning to you."

So it was that the greedy hunters were forgiven. They never, ever again took more game than they needed. They remained very respectful of animals, birds and of the Little People.

How Meat Became Food

Slave Legend

When the delicate balance among Creator's creatures is disturbed, traditional ways of life change.

Before the People arrived on Mother Earth, all the birds, animals and fishes spoke the same language. They were all vegetarians and most of all, they were all good friends.

But then a big snow came. It snowed for many Round Moons and the snow covered all the plants, making it very difficult to find food. Many animals and birds perished from starvation. Even the fish People were having problems with the ice, it was so thick they had to stay in very deep water.

One day, the Leader of the animals and birds, Wolf, called a Council of all the remaining creatures. It was decided to ask the Sky People what was causing it to snow continuously.

At the Council, one of every kind of animal and bird was chosen to go to the Sky People to try to sort out the problem and to get things back to normal.

The animals were carried by the birds to their destination and so it was that this Grand Delegation reached the Sky World. As they entered the gates, Sun began to shine on a wonderful lake. The Sky World was truly a beautiful place. Guarding the entrance was a huge lodge. However, everyone was horrified when they realized the lodge was covered with skins from dead animals.

Suddenly, two fairly small animals emerged from the Lodge and bid all welcome. These animals were unknown to the Earth animals at that time. The animals in question were a black-brown in color and had pointed snouts with very sharp teeth and claws. They were, in fact, Bear cubs.

"Come in," said the pair and the Delegation went in the lodge. The lodge belonged to Black Bear and her two cubs. As I have said Bear was a species of animal not yet settled on Mother Earth.

Wolf addressed the cubs, "We have come from the World below, Mother Earth. We wish to know why the snow is constantly falling and Father Sun has stopped shining?"

The young cubs, looking rather apprehensive, told the Delegation, "We are just young Bears, we don't know the answers to your questions. Our mother is out hunting and will return soon. She may have the explanation."

"What is hunting?" asked Wolf.

"She has gone to catch animals, hopefully a tasty Caribou, so we may eat," said one of the cubs.

"You eat the flesh of Caribou?" exclaimed the horrified Caribou, "How disgusting. Why don't you eat plants like us?"

Then, looking up at the ceiling of the lodge, Caribou noticed strange-looking pieces of wood. One had a very sharp point on it. There were also Five Bags hanging there. One was wide open and hanging upside down. Snow was pouring from it, down through a hole onto Mother Earth below. Three of the other bags were open but not hanging upside down. The fifth bag was tightly bound and glowed strangely.

Ignoring the bags for the time being, Caribou asked, "What are those odd-looking pieces of wood for?"

One of the little Bears said, "One is a bow, the other a spear."

"What are they used for?" asked Wolf.

"They are to hunt with, to kill animals so they can be eaten," said one of the cubs. The whole Delegation let out a gasp of revulsion, then fell silent, looking at each other uneasily.

Wolf asked nervously, "What about the four bags. Are they filled with dead animals?"

"No," laughed the cubs and the smaller one explained, "Those are the elements for the Earth that you come from. One holds the Winds, another the Cold and Snow—that's the one that's hanging upside down. Another the Rain, that one the Fog and that one...." The small Bear hesitated, realizing it had already said too much. "I am sorry I cannot tell you. You will have to

 50

wait for my mother. She would be very angry if I said more. She may tell you but I cannot."

Wolf, the Grand Leader of the Delegation had listened to all that had been said and was now convinced the bag that glowed held the Mother Earth's Sun and that is what they had come for. He hustled all the Delegates outside and held yet another Council. He told them of his suspicions, that the last bag, the one that was glowing, contained Earth's Sun. They were planning how to steal it back when they saw the mother Black Bear pulling her canoe up on the bank of the beautiful lake. She was enormous and ferocious looking. But, thankfully, she was not carrying any dead animals.

"We must act quickly. I have a plan," said Wolf. "Beaver, go to the Bear's canoe and gnaw the handle of her paddle close to the blade. Chew it almost all the way through. When you have finished, signal Caribou. Then, Caribou, you must run out to the lake and go into the water. Swim away as fast as you can. I think you will be pursued by Bear. If her cubs spoke the truth, you are their favorite meal. If she chases you and gets too close, swim to shore and hide in the woods. While this is going on, I need volunteers to snatch the bag that contains our Sun."

Eagle, Crow, Fox and Mole said they would do the job. Wolf instructed them further, "When you get to the Bag That Glows, undo it and make sure Sun comes out. Turn the bag that holds Cold and Snow right-side up."

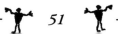

With the plans made, Beaver ran down to where Bear had left her canoe and chewed the paddle handle almost through. Meanwhile, Mother Bear came up from the lake without seeing Caribou enter the water. She was almost at her lodge when the cubs spotted Caribou swimming in the water. They cried out to her:

"Mother, mother, look. Caribou."

Mother Bear, seeing her prey, ran to her canoe, jumped in and pushing out from the bank. She began to stroke powerfully through the water after her quarry and was closing fast. Caribou was terrified and made a desperate sprint toward the shore and the safety of the trees. Just as Bear was about to overtake Caribou, her paddle broke, throwing her forward and causing her canoe to tip over, pitching the mother Bear into the lake. She was swallowed by the dark waters and drowned.

Caribou swam ashore and, with the others, ran to the lodge. Inside the four volunteers had pulled down the bag that Wolf had indicated. Mole had gnawed through the sinew that held it closed. Sure enough, it contained Earth's Sun. It shone so brightly, as it left the confines of the bag, that it almost blinded Mole. To this day Mole does not see well and his nose was singed and remains a bright pink .

Wolf, the Leader of the Delegation, took pity on the Bear cubs after their mother had been drowned and told them to come with them to the World below. Their task completed, the Delegation quickly left the Sky World.

When they got home, they could see that the snow was not quite so deep as when they had left. Sun was shining and the snow melting. It was much warmer and everyone was happy. They all ran around, even though the snow was still quite deep. In fact, it was still deep enough that they couldn't see properly where they were going.

A lot of accidents and mishaps occurred. Moose ran into a tree and squashed his nose and while he was holding it to ease the pain, he stood on Loon, flattening his back. Buffalo stepped on Beaver's tail and flattened it. Buffalo then bruised his back and a big hump formed. Blue Jay got stuck in the snow and his wings froze and turned bright blue. Cardinal cut himself on a sharp rock and his blood turned his feathers bright red. When he shook them, his blood went over Lynx and caused spots on the cat's fur. Worst of all, the two Black Bear cubs who liked to eat flesh were now on Earth and were getting very hungry.

The snow melted so fast that it wasn't long before the land was covered with water, so the animals and birds still could find no plants to eat. Wolf sent Raven, who in those days was the most beautiful of birds, to see if he could find land. He set Ducks to the task of pulling the land back from beneath the waters, so the creatures would have somewhere dry to stand.

Raven flew for many days and had found no land. One day, far below, he saw a small island. Upon it lay the corpse of Rabbit. The ravenous Raven, flew down and tore pieces of the rotting flesh from Rabbit's dead body, greedily devouring it.

When Raven returned, all the other animals were so disgusted with his behavior that they asked Creator to transform him into the bird he is today, a carrion eater, a scavenger, a bird of no grace or song.

Wolf, sent Ptarmigan out on a similar mission, to find land. Soon, she was back, carrying a small twig in her beak, signaling that there was land and plant food nearby. Ptarmigan was rewarded with the gift of an extra coat, a beautiful, pure white one, for the Winter. It was a coat to commemorate the animals' and birds' victory over the Winter of the Never-Ending-Snow. People, now, can always tell when Winter approaches by the white robe of Ptarmigan.

With Bears and Ravens seeking flesh for food, the peaceful Slave Lake area was not the same. It became a violent and barbarous place. Soon, other birds were attacking each other and eating the flesh of fish, other birds and small animals.

Even the great Leader, Wolf, killed others for food. Along came Man and there has been no peace ever since. The new order of things became hunt or be hunted because meat became food.

Mule

Lakota Legend

Love and devotion are qualities which Creator prizes in both His human and animal creations.

During one of the many skirmishes that were a part of the so-called Sioux Wars*, some Oglala Lakota captured many Mules and Horses from the Long Knife soldiers. The warriors and their booty arrived at their village. Dressed in their finest war clothing and paint, they showed off their new-found wealth.

After much dancing and boasting of brave deeds, the extra Horses and Mules that were not selected by the warriors were divided among the less fortunate People of the village. One of the Mules was given to an elderly lady, who appreciated the gift, but her beautiful granddaughter with whom she lived learned to value the Mule even more as it helped her considerably with her chores. The Mule and the young girl had become fast friends.

To be kind, generous and thoughtful of others are qualities much admired by all Lakota, and this young girl not only had these attributes, she had many, many more. She was the prettiest, no, the most stunning young woman that any Lakota could ever remember having had live among them. She was as beautiful inside as she was on the outside. The young woman had been brought up by her good and wise Grandmother with whom she still lived.

Of course, the young woman had many admirers. Many came to court her and many were turned away. One day, the most handsome, bravest warrior from the Clan came to court the beautiful maiden. She had shyly watched this fine, handsome man on many occasions, as they had grown up together. She knew him to be kind and generous, a person of good heart. She accepted him as a suitor and soon fell deeply in love with him. So, with her Grandmother's blessing, she wed the handsome warrior. Shortly thereafter, she bore him twin sons. The whole village was overjoyed at the great bounty Creator had bestowed on the handsome couple. There was much feasting and gaiety.

The young woman's Grandmother said to herself, "These good-looking babies will need cradle boards. I will make them from the finest materials." Which is what she did, presenting the young parents with not only the beautifully made cribs, but also with her Mule.

She said to them, "Here, take my gifts. Take this Mule, this gentle beast that my granddaughter greatly admires. It will carry your babies, one strung from each side in the cradle boards I have fashioned for you." With that said, she handed the reins to her granddaughter, who was positively beaming and making a great fuss of her old friend, Mule.

Mule seemed very happy with the new arrangement, especially when the young mother placed the twins in their cradle boards on each side of the beast. If it is possible for a Mule to look proud and happy, this one definitely did. During the many seasons that followed, the Mule took the children everywhere and was always as gentle and calm as it could be. It seemed to love just being near the babies.

Sometime later, the father was going on a hunting trip with some other warriors and decided to take his family along. He felt there would be little danger as they were going to hunt quite near to their own village. The next day at first light, his pretty wife brought the babies out in their cradle boards and was about to go and fetch her Mule when her husband picked up the boards and hung them on either side of his favorite War-Horse, saying, "Your Mule is not good enough for my fine sons! It can carry our cooking pots and pull our Lodge poles which is a much more fitting task for such an animal."

And so it was that his pretty wife packed the things they needed on the hunt and placed them on the Mule. She then slung a travois of lodge poles over his back to pull the heavy Buffalo skins that would cover the lodge and keep them warm.

As soon as she finished packing, the Mule went berserk. It bucked and kicked, smashing the lodge poles and strewing the family's belongings over a large area. Even the brave warriors could not get anywhere near the enraged animal as it jumped and kicked.

Grandmother came running up and, smiling, said, "Get the babies from your War Horse. Today you will learn something." The father did as he was told and the old woman walked bravely over to the Mule. It immediately calmed down as she soothed the creature by blowing softly into its nostrils, patting its neck and talking gently to it. In the meantime, the father had taken the babies in their cradle boards off his War-Horse's back and brought them to his grandmother.

"Put them on the Mule," she commanded.

"You cannot be serious, grandmother. This animal tried to kill me and my hunting companions," replied the father.

"Do as I bid. All will be well, trust me," she continued. He, cautiously, approached the Mule and placed the babies in their cradle boards over the animal's back. The Mule became very peaceful and looked happy and content. Grandmother spoke out, saying, "You see, this Mule wants to be the traveling companion of the babies. It feels that it is their protector. If I were you, I would let it do just that."

And so it was, the small hunting party set off with the babies slung from the Mule and their father's War-Horse pulling the travois. When they were about one Sun's traveling time from their village, they set up a make-shift camp and settled down for the night.

Just before Sun came up, they were attacked by Crow warriors. Luckily, though, the Lakota had posted a sentry who managed to sound the alarm. The Lakota poured out of their lodges, ready to fight their enemies. A great melee ensued, with bustling, bravado and counting of coup. While the battle was going on, the young woman got her twins into their cradle boards and onto the Mule's back, driving the beast out from amongst the bitter antagonists. The Lakota Warriors fought hard and, eventually, drove the Crow away with very little bloodshed on either side.

After the skirmish, the young couple searched for the Mule and their babies but found nothing. It was with heavy hearts that they concluded the twins must have been captured or killed by the Crow. The heart-broken couple bade farewell to their companions who were getting organized to chase the Crow back to their own lands, promising to make them pay for the outrage. The parents headed back to their village, both singing Death Songs for their poor babies.

Imagine their joy when they approached the village and saw the old Mule grazing outside their Grandmother's lodge, the cradle boards still hanging on either of its sides. Their Grandmother was sitting in front of their lodge with the twins, one perched on each of her legs. The old lady was happily cooing at the pair as she bounced them up and down. The young couple was ecstatic to see the youngsters and their brave protector, the Mule.

The warrior never again doubted the animal and, from then on, it always carried the babies whenever they needed to be moved. In fact, as they grew, both boys learned to ride on the beast's back. They often rode double, with old Mule seemingly happy anytime the boys saw fit to be near it.

Later, as the boys matured and were given Buffalo Ponies, they gave up riding the old Mule. It seemed with all the hunting, courting, and warring with the Long Knife soldiers and the Crow, they had forgotten their friend.

One day their father turned the elderly, but certainly still healthy, Mule out to pasture and promised his wife that it would do no more work for the family. "This brave beast deserves some time to itself. We will look after it well," he said. Shortly thereafter, seemingly without reason, the Mule died. It is said that the animal so loved the twins that not to serve them and be near them had broken its heart.

*This story occurred shortly after the White Man Soldiers arrived on the Plains. Gold had been found in the Black Hills. The Bozeman Trail had been cut through the Lakota lands, affording would-be settlers a way West. The ensuing Sioux Wars were believed to have led to the Centennial Campaign, George Custer's annihilation at the Little Bighorn and the ultimate defeat of the Plains Native People.

Runner

Cherokee Legend

The fleetest of the forest gets a new name.

The forest was tinder dry, because there had been no rain for two Round Moons. It was the first baby for the young mother. As you can imagine, it was very difficult to find food in the parched forest. In fact she had hardly found enough to feed herself, let alone her yet unborn child. She now lay in a clearing away from the main herd and waited for her baby to come.

"Ah, there's my baby," she watched as the little one arrived on Earth Mother. A brand new Runner had been born, a little girl. The little one was very pretty, but very small. "I hope she lives. Without rain none of us will."

She closed her eyes. "Please Creator, help her through her first days," she prayed. The young mother leant down to lick the tiny child clean. As she did so, she heard the first raindrops hit the forest canopy. All the Runners below looked to the Heavens, giving silent thanks for the gift of the life-giving rain.

Two days later the forest had been renewed and the Runner child was still alive. The new mother again gave thanks to Creator. Her baby's body was tiny and her long legs very wobbly. She had an awful time trying to walk, let alone run, she complained to her mother.

"Why would they call me Runner? I can't even walk!" cried her child.

"Patience, little one," her mother responded. "Eventually you will be as I am, one of the fastest and most agile creatures in the forest."

"I don't think so, Mother. My legs are far too long. I wish this Creator person you keep praying to would shorten them," said the disgruntled child

Unbeknown to the Runners below, Creator had watched the birth of the child and had answered her mother's prayers with rain. He heard the small Runner's queries and decided to pay a visit. He walked up to the herd of Runners, who instinctively knew it was Creator and bowed in homage. Creator waved them up and shook His head, smiling at the cowering animals.

"No need for any bowing. Up. Up. I have come to talk to the new one among you." He walked over to where the little one stood, wobbling next to her mother, and spoke directly to her. "So you don't like your legs, little one?"

The child was embarrassed and tried to hide under her mother. "What's that Creature doing here?" she asked her mother.

 62

"Don't be rude, child. That is our Creator. He wants to talk to you—come out and answer His question."

The baby shyly looked out from under her mother.

"Creator, my legs are too long for my body. I can't even walk properly, yet I'm called Runner. I look ridiculous." Creator laughed out loud.

"You do not look ridiculous. You are beautiful, little one," Creator said, then thought for a moment and continued. "Let me tell you of a few of the birds and animals that didn't like the way they were made at first but later changed their minds." He sat on a nearby fallen tree and continued: "One of them was Owl. Those big eyes, Owl didn't like them at all, but soon found them very useful, providing night vision and easy food gathering."

"I'd like to have big eyes," requested the child.

"You do," said Creator.

Creator again addressed the small Runner: "I will tell you another story. This one concerns Rabbit. When I created him, he did not like his long ears, but soon he realized that those ears he hated afforded him great hearing. A much-needed gift for one who is a food source for many."

"I wish I had long ears," said the youngster.

"You do, little one," said her mother.

"I don't like my legs, but I do like these stories, Creator. Tell me more."

"All right. This one concerns Buzzard. When I made Buzzard, he stood before me covered with fine, soft, fluffy down. I had made him a beautiful

robe of dark brown feathers, but unfortunately I had made the neck hole too small. As I pulled the robe down over his head, it yanked out all of his small downy feathers. I also elongated his neck and left him as he looks today, a long-necked, bald-headed bird. I became quite angry when other birds and animals laughed at him. I was sorry for what I had done to Buzzard and decreed, 'From this day, all of you that laughed at him will supply him with food.' From that time to this Buzzard has never had to hunt for food."

"That's a great story. Tell some more, Creator," demanded the Runner.

"I will tell you one more, child, then I must go." He moved around a little, getting Himself comfortable. After that was achieved He began a new story. "There is a bird called Meadow Lark. She, like you, hated her long legs. Even more, she hated her long feet. One day some time back, those feet saved her life. You see, there was a very strong wind and she was caught up in it. It was her long feet that allowed her to hold on tight to a tree limb, saving her life. You see, child, everything that I have given to the birds and animals is for a reason. Your long legs will soon serve you well."

"Well, if You promise that my legs will get stronger, I will keep them," conceded the precocious child. Creator smiled, knowing the sassy, tiny Runner would one day be a great leader.

"I will give you something, child. You will be the fastest of all the Creatures of the forest. Runner, You now have a New Name. From this day forth, you will be called Deer."

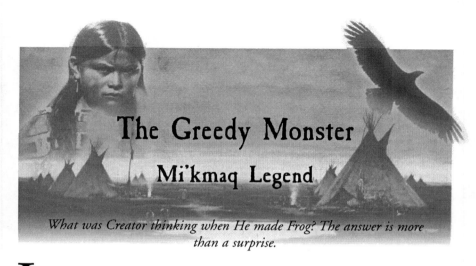

The Greedy Monster

Mi'kmaq Legend

What was Creator thinking when He made Frog? The answer is more than a surprise.

It had not rained for a very long time and most of the streams had dried up. The animals and People were having a hard time. The stream that had flowed past the People's village was dry. The People didn't know what to do as they relied on it for all their water. The Elders sent their best warrior to see if there was anything blocking the water. Perhaps Beaver had dammed it.

The warrior went off on his mission, but was soon back. He told the Elders, "There is a dam further upstream, but no Beaver built this dam. There are warriors guarding it. They told me that their chief wants all the water behind the dam for himself."

The People were very angry. The Elders held Council. At the meeting, the War Chief said, "Without water, all our People will die. If we are to die anyway, it is better to fight." So it was decided to go to war against the greedy Chief's People, those who had dammed the stream.

A War-Party was formed. They bade good-bye to the Elders and, under the guidance of the War Leader, they went to do battle against the stealers of the life-giving water. When the warriors got to the dam, a few crept stealthily up on the sentinels and quickly subdued them. The main body of Mi'kmaq went around the dam to where they thought the Chief might be camped. There were only a few guards there and they were quickly dispatched.

The Mi'kmaq, let out whoops of victory. Suddenly, a huge Monster arose from the lake. Its huge, dull green mouth gaped open, a black disgusting tongue flicked in and out of its cavernous mouth. Its stringy fingers were webbed together. As the Monster arose, the braves could see its huge, bloated yellow belly. Its whole body was covered in green slime. The Mi'kmaq had no chance against the giant Monster, and he made short work of the horrified braves. He had soon killed all but one, the warrior who had first been sent to the dam. He ran for his life back to the village with the terrible news.

The People fell into panic. Most of the young warriors from the village were dead. There was hardly anyone left to do battle with the Monster. The old Chief told the People to Pray to Creator. They sent Tobacco Smoke and Prayers, asking for guidance from Great Spirit. Eagle took the Prayer Smoke to Creator, Who felt sorry for the Mi'kmaq in their time of need. He sent word to Koluscap (Trickster) to go to their aid.

"Koluscap, I want you to do battle for the Mi'kmaq. Deliver these People from the grips of the Monster. Restore their water," commanded Creator.

When Koluscap appeared in the village, He showed Himself in Human form. He had two Wolves, one on either side. The one that ran at His right was white, and the one at His left was pitch black. His face was painted white on the left side and black on the other. He carried Eagle on His shoulder. He was a fine-looking warrior, tall and elegant, but it was also a fearsome guise. He carried a war club made from the root of a birch tree.

When Koluscap entered the Mi'kmaq village, the People knew He must have been sent by Creator to save them. "You are welcome, Handsome Stranger," they said. "We will gladly feed You but we cannot give You water. A Monster upstream has dammed our water supply and will not give us any. We did battle with Him and, alas, He has killed nearly all our young men."

"I do not need your food; thank you for offering. Direct Me to the Monster. I will soon get your water flowing again."

The Mi'kmaq did as He asked and told Koluscap that they would Pray for His safe return.

There was a very bad smell as Koluscap made His way to the dam of the Monster. Flies were everywhere. The terrible odor was caused by the dead and rotting flesh of the warriors, fish, turtles, and other water creatures that the Monster, through his greed, had killed. Koluscap finally arrived at the dam, which was still guarded by the remnants of the Monster's warriors.

Koluscap walked right up to them and demanded, "Give Me some water, so I may quench my dry throat."

"We have none to spare," came the booming reply from somewhere behind the guards. "Go away now or I will kill You."

The guards were not quite as hard-hearted and gave Koluscap a small bark cup of muddy water.

"This will not do," shouted Koluscap, throwing the water on to the ground. The guards motioned Him to be silent, fearing for His life and theirs if their Monster-Leader became upset. Koluscap didn't care. He shouted again, "I said this will not do, you Greedy, Ugly Green Object."

"Who dares call me ugly?" roared the Monster as he rose from the water.

"I called you ugly, but I had not seen you. Now that I have, you are even more repulsive than I imagined. You're fat, too, and, that color of green makes you look like you're about to vomit."

Well, as I'm sure you can imagine, the Monster was beside himself with rage. "How dare You speak to me like that. You are about to be torn limb from limb...." ranted and raved the Monster. In response, Koluscap stamped His feet. Each time He did, He grew bigger and bigger. Soon, He was bigger than the trees that surrounded the dam. He lifted one of His feet and slammed it down upon the dam, sending the guards scurrying for their lives.

"Chase them, My Wolves, make sure they never return to the Land of the Mi'kmaq," he commanded. Koluscap's foot had breached the dam, causing the waters to gush from the break and leaving the Monster stranded in the middle, flopping around in the mud.

Koluscap's club had grown along with Him. He brought it down with a pulverizing blow, crushing the rest of the dam for all time. He knelt down and scooped up the Monster, who was now no bigger than Koluscap's hand. Koluscap gripped him tightly, causing the Monster's eyes to bulge from their sockets and his back legs to bend in very strange shapes.

"You are very greedy, You Ugly Pest, You must learn to share." Koluscap stamped His feet and He began to get smaller. As He shrank, so did the Monster. Finally, Koluscap was again the size of a Mi'kmaq warrior. The Monster had shrunk to the size of Koluscap's hand. Koluscap loosened His grip and placed the not-so-big Monster on the earth.

"This will be your size and shape from this day. Your eyes will bulge and your back legs will remain bent the way they are now," proclaimed Koluscap. "For all the death you caused among the water creatures, you will live on flies and insects from now on, the way they live on the corpses you created. You will be called Bullfrog, and you will be hunted in water and on the land."

From that day to this, Bullfrog has kept himself hidden away. His song is one of sorrow for his greediness. Some say he still sings, "Give him none." But what he is saying is really, "Give, give." Bullfrog is still trying to make amends for what he did, fearful that Koluscap might return.

Five Round Moons of Winter and How Dog Joined Man

OjiCree Legend

Compromise was an important lesson among Native Peoples, but some creatures find their own solutions.

A long time ago after another particularly long, hard Northern Winter which some of the animals and birds loved and others hated, there was a great deal of discussion about what length Winter should be. Wisakachak gathered up the creatures to determine how many Round Moons Winter should last.

All the animals and birds were there. Of course, the Water People were represented as were the Little People of the Air (insects).

"Well," said Wisakachak (Trickster), "How long should Winter be?"

"Well," said Ahtic (Caribou), "I love Winter. I think it should be all the time."

"I agree," said Mooswa (Moose), "I think Winter should last one Round Moon for every hair on my body. I just love Winter. I don't have to put up with those stupid Pa Koo Shoh (Black Flies) and the rest of their nasty, blood-sucking family."

A groan of protest went out from the gathering. The moan of disapproval was from all who thought that idea incredibly stupid, especially the insects.

"Can you imagine Winter being all the time?" said Shingahdamequan (Turtle), in a small, disbelieving nervous tone.

"If Winter were all the time, Ahtic," said the wise Wisakachak. "The snow would be so deep that you would never be able to find food. And you, Mooswa, you have that over-sized warm coat I made for you, so, I guess you don't care about the cold. But you should. There must be a balance of Seasons. Just think of all the fine, succulent plants that you find in the rivers during Summer. Would you not miss them?"

Mooswa's expression changed to one of longing as he thought of his favorite pastime—eating.

"Well," said Amik (Beaver), "I like Winter. I get a warm, thick coat and there are always plenty of branches and twigs in my dam in the village where I live. I think Winter should be at least eight Round Moons long."

"That is all very well, Amik," said the perceptive Wisakachak, "but the ice could become so thick that you could freeze to death. The trees you need to feed yourself would not grow nearly as well without the warming of our Earth Mother in Summer ."

"I think it should be Summer all the time," croaked O Muhkuhke (Frog). "That way, I would be able to catch delicious flies all year 'round. I love Pa Koo Shoh and all their kin. They're yummy." Frog looked hungrily at the insect delegation who nervously looked away.

This comment upset the insects but, they knew they were safe and that Wisakachak would not allow any harm to come to them at the Council. Wisakachak addressed the ever-hungry Frog. "But if we had no Winter, O Muhkuhke, there would not be enough water to fill your pond and you would dry up and die," said the all-knowing Wisakachak.

Muskwa (Bear) spoke up saying, "I hate Winter, so I sleep through it. By the time it is over, I am so hungry that I am almost dead. I think, O Muhkuhke, almost has the right idea. Let's cut Winter to, say, four Round Moons, that's plenty."

Wisakachak said, "I think you are close, Muskwa. But, let's compromise. There are 13 Round Moons in the Summer-to-Winter cycle. Perhaps, we will have five Round Moons of Winter, one-and-a-half Round Moons of Spring, one and-a-half of Fall and five Round Moons of Summer. That would be a good compromise," said the very smart Wisakachak. And this was the

 72

arrangement all the animals, birds, insects and People of the water agreed to. All save one.

"I don't care how long winter is," said, Maheengun (Wolf) addressing the gathered creatures lazily. "I am fed up with this hard life we lead. I'm going to live with the People. I will sit by their warm fires and beg for food. I will go with them to their trap lines and live on scraps."

To which the gathering said, "They will be afraid of you. They will not accept you."

"I will make them welcome me into their village," snarled Wolf.

Muskwa warned, "They may take their anger and frustration out on you. They may abuse you, Maheengun."

"I don't care, I will make them love me. I will hunt for them," retorted Wolf in a whining voice. "And what's a little slap or kick now and then if you're getting well fed?"

"If the People allow you to join them, you will be despised by all the other animals," cautioned Wisakachak.

"I don't care. At least I will be warm and well fed," barked Maheengun. "I don't really care for any of you anyway."

From that day forward, Wolf joined Man and was known as Uhnemoosh (Dog) by the People. Dog has remained a constant companion, even though the odd kick or slap does come his way.

Beautiful Fire Keeper
Nisqually Legend

Among the Nisqually, the greed of two brothers is credited with the creation of America's most famous volcano.

A long time ago, the land where the Nisqually lived was always warm and pleasant. There was always lots to eat and the animals and birds gave themselves freely. Creator provided for all their needs and everyone was happy.

Two boys were born into a good family, a family of Leaders. They grew up with great strength, but very little wisdom. They both wanted control. They both wanted power, not just over the People, but also over the land that they lived upon. Each brother garnered men who would support his claims, men who would speak out against the rights of the opposing brother. They were men who would fight to support those supposed rights. For the first time the People talked of killing each other.

Creator was furious with the brothers. In a Dream, Creator showed them both a new land, a land of great beauty. He then spoke to them, "Tomorrow, you will be guided to the place I showed you in your Dreams. You will both take a bow and one arrow. When you have reached the place, each of you in turn will shoot your arrow. Where it lands is where you will take the People that will follow you. That is where you will live; and you will live, hopefully, in peace."

The next morning, the brothers arose early. Taking their bows and one arrow each, they set off on their quest. They came to a beautiful river that both remembered from their Dreams. As they argued over who should shoot first, Creator's voice boomed down.

"The eldest of you will shoot first and wherever the arrow falls, will be his Land."

The eldest of the brothers pulled his bow taut and fired his arrow right over the river. Where it landed is where his People went. The other brother fired his arrow to the North and he and his followers settled where it landed. Before the brothers and their People had set off for their new lands, Creator made a stone crossing over the river. Then he said, "As long as your hearts are good toward each other, this crossing will always join your Peoples. It will be a Symbol of Peace."

And so, for a time, the People remained happy crossing freely to visit and help each other. Soon, the brothers again wanted more. The younger brother said, "It was not fair my brother got to shoot his arrow first. He chose

to shoot his arrow at the Land that I wanted for my People. It is far more beautiful there and the hunting is much better." He soon had his followers all riled up again.

Creator saw what was going on and knew that war would soon be declared if he didn't intervene. He decided to send rain to cool off and dampen the spirits of the trouble-makers. It rained so hard it extinguished all the People's fires, but one, the fire of the hermit Loo-Wit.

Without fire the People could not cook or warm themselves. Everyone became soggy, damp and downright miserable. The People Prayed to Creator to forgive them for their thoughts of greed and war, even the brothers Prayed for forgiveness. Creator, feeling benevolent, decided to help the brothers and their People one more time. He went to the hermit, Loo-Wit, who was getting on in years and who owned the only fire still burning.

"Loo-Wit," said Creator, "you are a good, wise woman, and have not engaged in any of this war-like activity. I will give you whatever you wish for if you share your fire with the People. I hope and Pray they will finally come to their senses."

Loo-Wit thought for some time about Creator's generous offer. Finally, she said, "I would enjoy my beauty returning to me. I would like to be a young woman again."

"So be it. Your wish is granted," said Creator. Loo-Wit was immediately as beautiful as she had been many years before. Creator said, "Tomorrow you

must take this fire to the river where the crossing lays. Let all the People who want fire have it. Tell all that take the fire that they must remain at peace."

The next morning at first light, Loo-Wit got up. Taking her heavy pack of dry wood and kindling and a firebrand from her hearth, she set off for the river crossing. Creator had made a beautiful day. Father Sun shone brightly and the Sky was the deepest blue. Loo-Wit was glad to see Sun again as it had been a long time since He had shone.

When she arrived, she set up her fire, then called to the People to come and help themselves. The People heard her calling and came out of their lodges. They saw the beautiful day and the beautiful woman calling to them to come and get the badly needed, warming fire. Soon, the People came and took the fire, and Loo-Wit told them Creator's Message of Peace.

When younger brother saw the beautiful Loo-Wit, he immediately fell in love with her and asked her to marry him. At around the same time, the older brother arrived to partake in the fire give-away. He, too, fell in love with Loo-Wit. Like his brother, he asked for her hand in marriage.

Loo-Wit considered the brothers' marriage offers. The fact was, she didn't like either of them very well. "Sure they are handsome," she thought. "But they are also ruthless and greedy."

The brothers were growing tired of waiting to see who Loo-Wit would choose and sent emissaries to ask her to hurry up and decide. She sent the messengers back, telling them that she did not wish to marry either of them.

When the brothers got her message, each took it to mean Loo-Wit was about to marry the other. Each became angry and sent war parties to attack the other's camp.

Creator was watching all of this. Finally, He had had enough. In His fury, He turned both brothers into mountains. The younger brother He made into the mountain the White Man calls Mount Adams; the eldest into Mount Hood. He destroyed the crossing over the river and made the river very narrow where the stone bridge had been.

Loo-Wit was very unhappy, blaming herself for the friction between the brothers. Thinking her beauty had caused most of the trouble, she Prayed to Creator to change her back to an old woman. Creator heard her Prayers and knew that the friction between the brothers was not her fault. Instead of turning her back into an old woman, He turned her into a beautiful mountain, much more stunning than the mountains He had created from the ever-feuding brothers.

He made her into a Fire-Keeper for all time. She became what the White Man calls Mount St. Helen. She still sits between the quarrelsome brothers and she sleeps soundly most of the time. But if Creator becomes unhappy or angry over the lack of concern that People—White or Red—have in their dealings with Mother Earth, Loo Wit will awaken and spread her fire of destruction which is Creator's wrath.

Bear's Fat

OjiCree Legend

Taking advantage of others can often lead to disappointment.

Wisakachak (Trickster) had grown very lazy and never wanted to hunt for Himself. One day, He was very hungry but felt it was just too much bother to search for food. "I wish someone would come along who had some food. Maybe I could trick them out of it," He thought. Then, He saw Muskwa (Bear) lumbering along. "My Brother," He always called everyone brother when He wanted something. "Do you have any food with you?"

"No," replied Muskwa. "I am on my way to the edge of the lake to eat Blueberries."

"Do you mind if I come along?" asked Wisakachak.

"Not at all, come on. I know where there is a big patch. The berries this Summer are very plump and good."

So, Wisakachak and Muskwa set off for the Blueberry patch. When they arrived, Muskwa sat down and began to devour the succulent fruit eagerly, consuming great numbers of them. Wisakachak was watching the chubby Bear, greedily gobbling the sweet berries. He thought what a grand meal that fat Muskwa would make, much better than these silly Blueberries. He would be something to get his teeth into. If only He could figure out a way of killing him without getting killed Himself.

Wisakachak said. "Look over there. That looks like a great spot for berries, doesn't it?"

Muskwa looked long and hard, squinting through half-closed eyes to where Wisakachak's outstretched finger was pointing.

You probably have figured out that there was no berry spot where He was pointing. Wisakachak was tricking Muskwa.

"I can't see it. My eyes must be getting bad," said Muskwa. "I hope it is a good spot, for the berries here are almost all gone. I wish I could see the place clearly that you are pointing at. I am still very hungry. I just can't see what you can see. It just looks like bare rocks to me."

"Your eyes must be getting bad, I can clearly see plenty of Blueberry bushes. You know, when I have trouble with my eyes I put Blueberry juice into them."

"Blueberry juice? Does that help you see better?" asked Muskwa in an incredulous, but serious, voice.

"Oh yes," said the sly Wisakachak. "It hurts at first, but it will clear your eyes. You will be able to see for a very long way."

So, Muskwa allowed Wisakachak to squeeze Blueberry juice into his eyes. It stung so badly that Muskwa did a little dance of pain and soon became very dizzy. Meanwhile, Wisakachak looked around for a suitable piece of wood to use as a club to beat the blinded Muskwa into Bear steaks.

After Wisakachak had killed Muskwa, He prepared racks over a fire and cut Bear's flesh into pieces ready for cooking. As the flesh slowly heated through, the fat began to run. Wisakachak collected it in a Birch bark container as the fat was one of His favorite things to eat. As the bark container filled, He poured the contents into a cleaned bladder He had taken from Muskwa's stomach.

At last, Wisakachak's meal was almost ready. "I will save this fat to eat at a later time. I must find a place for my bladder of fat, a place where the animals can't get at it," He thought.

Nearby, there were some tall trees. Wisakachak climbed one and hung His prized fat on one of the high branches. As He descended, His loincloth got tangled the lower limbs and He got stuck. He couldn't move. The more He struggled, the tighter the tree held Him captive.

Suddenly, out of the bush loped three, ever-hungry, (Maheengun) Wolves. They looked up in the tree and then at the Bear meat. Seeing that Wisakachak was firmly stuck, pardon the pun, they wolfed down the Bear meat and quickly left.

The angry Wisakachak struggled and struggled. Finally, His breechcloth broke and the now-naked Wisakachak climbed back up the tree to retrieve His bladder of fat which was all He had left to eat. On His way down, He retrieved His breach cloth.

Wisakachak walked towards the lake, still annoyed at the thieving Wolves. "Why don't Wolves catch their own food? Mangy mutts," He shouted. He realized the fat in the bladder had not congealed properly, as the weather was too hot, and when the fat was runny, it was not good to eat. He was wondering how to harden the fat when Wachusk (Muskrat) swam by.

"Wachusk, will you tow this bladder around the lake for Me? I need the fat in it to harden. If you do as I ask, I will give you some."

And, Wachusk agreed.

"You must dive deep, My friend. It will need the cold, lower waters to harden the fat." Wisakachak tied the fat bladder to Wachusk's tail and off he swam, diving deep under the waters of the lake while trying to cool the fat in the bladder.

"Is it hard yet?" inquired Wisakachak as Wachusk surfaced.

"Not yet," said Wachusk and then continued. "I'm not sure if even the lower waters are cold enough to congeal the fat. The Summer has been so hot this year."

"Try again," instructed Wisakachak. "I am very hungry. If the fat doesn't harden, We will just have to eat it runny."

Wachusk raised her head out of the water, ready to dive deeply; however, the bladder had become entangled on a half-submerged branch. When Wachusk plunged under the waves, the bladder broke free and burst on top of the water, spewing its greasy contents on the surface.

Wisakachak was exasperated. It seemed to Him He would never get a meal this day. To add to His distress, Amik (Beaver) swam up and started eating the fat on top the water.

Before He could frighten Beaver off, Mooswa (Moose) jumped into the lake and swam out, joining in the fat feast. Even Wachusk joined in, which is why that even today these animals have a lot of fat on their bodies. The last straw came when Waboose (Rabbit) came hopping out of the bush and was about to swim out to help himself to Wisakachak's fat.

Wisakachak grabbed Rabbit and flung him into the water. Wouldn't you know it, Waboose landed in the middle of the remaining grease and swam around in it with just his head poking out of it. Even to this day, Waboose has fat only around its neck from the time he was thrown into Bear's grease.

Wisakachak was still very hungry, so He went back to where Muskwa had shown Him the Blueberries and had a little something to eat. He vowed to get even with the thieving animals.

Changing of Seasons
Iroquois Legend

The cycle of the Seasons is a never-ending one, as illustrated by the relationship of the characters in this story.

I f you had seen the Man, it would have been obvious to you that He was very old. His hair was pure white, as were the robes He proudly wore. His shoulders stooped a little as He slowly walked through the forest, beneath the cold, gray-black clouds that hid Father Sun. The Old Man's breath turned everything in His path to ice. Today, He felt His age. He was exhausted.

Four Round Moons back, the Old Man had caused the leaves on the trees to wither and die. Soon after, most of the birds fled from Him, escaping to the South. The Deer had retreated deep into the forest to avoid His wrath. Even mighty Bear could not deal with this harsh, ruthless the Old Man. Instead, Bear dug a den and hid. Very few animals appreciated the Old Man's austere contributions to their lives. But to those few who did, Old Man gave beautiful gifts of pure white robes, much like His own.

While the Old Man stayed in the Land of the Iroquois, His only friend was North Wind. They would sit together in the Old Man's lodge and talk and laugh for days on end, but only about matters pertaining to Winter and cold. They never mentioned Sun, Summer or warmth.

One day, the North Wind sighed and softly said to His comrade, "You are looking very old, My Friend. It seems just a few Round Moons ago You were so young."

"Yes, I know. It will soon be time for Me to leave," said the Old Man, sadly shaking His head.

Soon after, while the Old Man was walking through the forest checking on things, He noticed a crack in the ice on the river. The Old Man tried to blow His cold breath to seal it. But all He could manage was a few short puffs. His old body could not produce enough cold to complete the task. He called the North Wind to come and close the fracture.

"Fix that crack right away," He demanded. "We don't want any of the Water Spirits waking up and getting restless, just because they see a break in the ice. I have at least half a Moon left to go." The North Wind complied with the Old Man's order. On His way back to His lodge, the Old Man couldn't help but notice that the snowdrifts seemed to be getting smaller. "I am getting very weary. Soon, I will have to give up," He thought.

Very early one morning not long after that, a young, handsome Man dressed in green and gold came knocking at the Old Man's lodge. "I have come for You, My Partner. Are You willing to go with Me for Your last walk?"

"Yes, I am ready. Let's go, My Young Friend," said the Old Man who was now walking very slowly with the aid of a staff. He listlessly followed the Young Man into the forest.

As the Old Man shuffled along, Father Sun came out from behind the dark gray clouds. As They walked on through the warmth of the new day, Old Man started to sweat profusely. It seemed He was in a dire state. His breath now came in very short gasps. He started to stumble. The Young Man just looked on and did nothing to help the Old One. He just smiled knowingly. The Old Man staggered a few more steps, then collapsed onto the forest floor.

Behind the Two Men where they had walked through the melting snow, beautiful, delicate flowers had sprung to life in the indentations left by Their moccasins.

"Good-bye, My Friend," said the Young Man, as the brave Old Man's life gently slipped away into the Sun-warmed ground.

Old Man Winter had been vanquished by Young Man Spring. But Creator would have Winter return again as a Youthful Man, as soon as it was time for that Season to renew the Circle of Life and Death in the Land of the Iroquois.

 86

Absaroke (Crow) Creation Story

Crow Legend

Absaroke creation legend that explains the interrelationship between Man, animals and Mother Earth.

Coyote, Creator's Helper surveyed all that had been established and was not happy. It was a very wet, damp World that now existed, a World that was covered with a vast Ocean.

"I wish I wasn't alone. There seems to be nothing here but Ocean. If I had the right building materials, I would create someone to share this world with Me," He thought. "I really could use a friend."

Just then, His request seemed to be answered. A pair of water birds appeared from nowhere and swam to him, peering at Him inquisitively with their bright, black eyes. Coyote was very pleased to see them and they chatted for a while.

"What are you called?" inquired Coyote.

"We don't know" replied the birds.

"Then I will name you," Coyote paused, "Ducks—that's what you will be called. Have you seen any other life while you were paddling around?" asked Coyote.

"No," they replied. "We've seen nothing at all. It seems there is just You and us. But we have often wondered what lays beneath these waters."

"Well, if you think there may be something down there, why don't you dive down and see what it could be," asked Coyote.

"What's diving?" the Ducks asked. Coyote described the action in detail. The Ducks had not thought of diving before, even though most Ducks now do it regularly. One of the Ducks, who was a little obstinate and maybe a little cowardly too, said, "I'm certainly not diving. I've never done it before. It's probably very dangerous. I could drown."

"I'm not frightened," said the other. "I'll do it. It sounds like fun."

"Good. Well done," said Coyote. "Perhaps you will find something of interest below the surface. If you do find anything, bring it up, so we can all look at it." And so the brave Duck dove down, leaving the not-so-brave Duck floating on the surface near Coyote.

Down below the surface, the other Duck swam deeper and deeper to explore what lay benieth. He was gone for a long time and Coyote began to worry that the fearful Duck may have been correct in his outlook.

"I hope your friend is all right," said Coyote, peering into the deep waters. "Maybe you were right. It is too dangerous. It's been a long time since he went under."

"I, too, am worried. He has never done this diving before. What will I do? He is my only friend and I fear he may have drowned," said Duck who had remained. "I don't think my friend can hold his breath for this long, even though he is a very good swimmer on the surface. Maybe...."

The fearful Duck had not finished his sentence, when rings appeared on the surface of the waters, heralding the return of the very brave, now Diving Duck. After he had surfaced, he swam quickly toward Coyote and his non-diving companion. In his beak, he carried a big scoop of mud which he deposited on one of Coyote's feet.

"Ah, so there is something down there!" exclaimed Coyote. "This, My Feathered Friends, is building material. I will show you something of great interest, now that you have brought this gift to Me." With that, He blew on the mud. It started to get thicker. He blew again and it expanded in all directions and soon became quite large. The Ducks were very impressed as now they could stand on this newly-created muddy island and keep their feet dry. Coyote blew again on the mud. Trees formed, grass began to grow. The little island began to get bigger and bigger.

"It is beautiful," said the Diving Duck.

"Yes, but it's very flat," said the fearful Duck who was also argumentative and always finding fault with something.

"Patience, My Friends. I am not finished yet," Coyote said as He took a branch from one of the newly-formed trees and scratched lines in the surface of the island. He then pushed earth around with his paws, forming peaks and dales. He again blew on the now-dry earth of the tiny island. It grew and grew, larger and larger. The scratches Coyote had made formed rivers and the mounded earth became mountains and valleys. The Ducks were even more impressed.

"It is beautiful. I cannot imagine a nicer-looking place," said the Diving Duck.

"It would be even nicer if there were more Ducks," said his non-diving, fearful, fault-finding, argumentative friend.

"You're right, though quite annoying," snapped Coyote, then in a nicer tone added, "I will make some friends for us all, so we will never be lonely." With that He took a little water and a little of the newly formed soil, mixed them and fashioned creatures. As He finished each one, He blew on it and it came to life.

First, He made Ducks just like the two that were with Him. Then He made Ducks of all varieties, males and females. He then instructed the newly-formed birds, with a big grin on His face, in what to do to create more Ducks. He made birds of every kind. He made Wolves and Foxes. Then He made the bigger animals, Buffalo, Musk-Ox, Caribou and all the animals of the World. He made insects. He made the fishes and mammals that would live beneath the waters of His rivers, lakes and seas. With one final puff, the task was done—Mother Earth was as we now know Her.

Coyote smiled and took another handful of earth and a little water. The Ducks wondered what else He could create. When He was done mixing and shaping, Coyote blew softly on His new creation. There before Him stood a very pretty, girl Coyote. When she saw Coyote beaming at her, He looked so friendly and kind that she fell in love with Him, even though she didn't know who He was.

"Who are You?" she asked coyly.

"I am Coyote. I created you to be My friend," He replied. "That is, if you like Me," He added sheepishly, well, as sheepish as a Coyote can be.

They became good friends and then good lovers. Pretty soon, they had small Coyotes to look after.

Some time later they were sitting around their fire after the little ones had gone to sleep. "You are very clever Coyote, but You haven't made anything new for a long time. Are You going to make anything else?" inquired His wife.

"Yes, I think so." He sat and thought for quite a while. Then, He stood up and said, "I will make Two-Legged People, People who will love and understand Mother Earth and all the animals and birds." With that said, He took earth and a little water and formed a Man. He then created a pretty, young Woman for the Man to love. After Coyote had put breath into the newly-made People, they came alive. Coyote addressed them.

"Always remember, the animals, birds and fishes are your brothers. Everything here is a Circle. Everything belongs," he said. "With Creator's blessing I have made this Beautiful World for you all to enjoy. Please use it wisely."

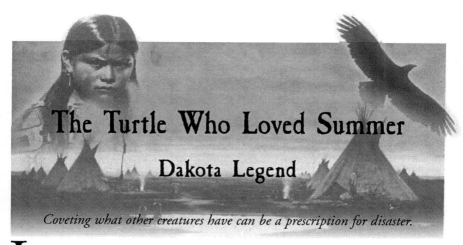

The Turtle Who Loved Summer

Dakota Legend

Coveting what other creatures have can be a prescription for disaster.

I t was the Moon of the Falling Leaves and Turtle knew soon snow would cover all the Land of the Dakota. He watched enviously as the birds gathered, getting ready for their long flight South. The birds had told Turtle many times about how warm it was in the South.

"Just like having two Summers," they said. "It's just lovely there, always lots to eat," they added. "Too bad Turtles can't fly," they laughed.

"Please, take me with you. Oh, please, please," implored Turtle, shivering, just thinking about the Winter to come. He was determined to go South with them.

"How can you come with us? You can't fly!" twittered the birds. "The very idea. Turtles flying, ha!"

"Oh, I so want to be where it is warm. I hate the snow. I can never find enough to eat. Please take me," he pleaded.

The birds had a kind Leader who said to Turtle, "Look here, Turtle. It really doesn't matter to me if you come. But, as it has been pointed out, you can't fly and it would be very difficult ...." the Leader broke off thinking to himself. Then he asked, "Could you hang on to a branch?"

"Oh, yes," answered Turtle. "I'm that kind of Turtle. A Snapping Turtle, the kind that can hang on to anything until I'm ready to let go. If I have a mind, I can just snap at a branch and hang on forever or break it in half. I would love to have an extra Summer. Please take me with you."

"Well, maybe we can take you, but it's a long way. Are you sure you can hang on?"

"As I said, when I bite onto something, I can lock my jaw," Turtle replied.

"Very well," said the Leader of the birds. He ordered a branch to be brought. "Now, Turtle, bite down in the middle of this branch and don't let go until we reach the Land of Summer."

Turtle did as he was told. Two big, strong birds took each end of the branch and slowly lifted Turtle into the air. At first, he was quite frightened. He was so high everything below looked minuscule. He saw many Buffalo; but from his altitude, they looked more like Ants.

They had not been flying for very long and already Turtle's jaw was beginning to ache. He wondered how much farther it was to the Land of Summer. So, he asked the birds who were carrying him how much longer the

trip would be. Of course, to enable him to talk to the birds, Turtle had to open his mouth. Alas, when he did, he let go of the branch. Down he came, plunging toward the Earth below.

He was so frightened that for the first time he pulled his head and legs inside his shell. Crunch...crash...bang were the sounds he made as he hit the ground. He bounced twice more before finally coming to rest. Turtle's shell was cracked and even though it healed, it still to this day has many scars and ridges. Turtle crept away to the nearest pond and dove in. Down to the very bottom he went, just as far as he could possibly get from the Sky, the vast Sky where the lucky birds can escape to the Land of Summer.

Turtle was so sore and tired from his ordeal that he slept all Winter, snug beneath the mud of the pond, and didn't come out until the next Spring.

It was nice and warm when Turtle finally emerged from his long hibernation. The Frogs already were singing their renewal songs, and the birds had returned and the nasty snow had gone. "Well," he thought, "even if I can't go to the Land of Summer, at least I slept through the cold, snowy Winter. I think that's what I will do from now on." And as we all know, to this day, that's exactly what he does.

Maid of the Mist

Seneca Legend

Many years ago, according to a Jesuit priest, the Seneca of the Iroquois Confederation gathered at Niagara Falls annually to make a sacrifice to the Spirits of the Great Waters.

In 1679, brave Chief Eagle's only daughter was going to die as a sacrifice to appease the Spirits of the Powerful Waters. His daughter was the prettiest of the young women of the Tribe, and had just reached womanhood. She was considered a fitting gift for the Spirits of Niagara Falls.

Chief Eagle loved his daughter with all his heart and his heart was heavy on hearing the news that his daughter had been chosen for the sacrifice. In fact, his heart was breaking. But his face showed none of the sadness he felt as he smiled in acknowledgment of the great Honor bestowed upon him and his beloved daughter.

Much grief had come to Chief Eagle in the past year. His loving wife had been killed in a raid by enemies of the Seneca. Now, his only daughter was to be sacrificed, leaving him alone in this World. It was more than he could endure.

Evening came and the Chief's pretty daughter was dressed in a beautiful, pure white buckskin dress. She was placed with reverence in a white canoe, along with fruit and other gifts for the Water Spirits. Although she was very frightened, she knew that it was a great Honor to be chosen.

And so it was, with a fearful heart, she began her journey, a journey of no return. The Seneca People fell silent as they watched from the bank. They saw her paddling toward the white waters and death. Suddenly, darting out from the darkness of the overhanging trees, came another canoe. The crowd strained their eyes to see who it was.

Then, Father Sun broke from behind a cloud and all was revealed. It was Chief Eagle. He was calmly, but swiftly, paddling to his cherished daughter's side. He had decided that he would be with her in death as well as life. He smiled at her as he reached her side, and held his canoe tightly to hers so they would cross over to the Spirit World together.

Hand in hand, over the edge of the cascading waters, they plunged together to their deaths on the jagged rocks and in the raging waters below. It is said she was transformed into the Maid of the Mist and he, the Ruler of the Crashing Waters.

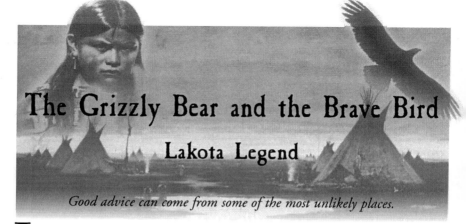

The Grizzly Bear and the Brave Bird

Lakota Legend

Good advice can come from some of the most unlikely places.

It was the Moon of the Black Cherries. Sitting Bull had gone hunting and had not yet reached his destination, the bend in the Arikara River—the place where the Deer came to drink. He was half walking, half climbing down a very steep slope through thick brush. It was quite windy and the tops of the waving trees below him were showing the light-colored underside of their leaves, making some of them look as though there was snow on them.

Sitting Bull stopped and yawned. He was very tired and his body craved sleep. Even so, he set off again, gradually descending to the river. As the terrain evened out near the water's edge, it became thick with trees. Now, all but the tops of the trees were shielded from the wind. He found a good, grassy clearing and decided to sleep for a while, He took off his quiver of arrows and put them on the ground with his bow, stretched and yawned again. Sitting Bull lay down on the soft grass and soon fell fast asleep.

Obviously, he did not know Grizzly Bear was foraging for roots, berries and mice nearby, or sleep would have been the furthest thing from his mind. Bear moved closer to where Sitting Bull was sleeping and was soon in the same clearing.

A pretty bird, a Yellow Throat, flew down and landed near where he soundly slept. It started to chirp and sing loudly. It sang while knocking its beak against the branch it was perched on. Of course, Sitting Bull awoke, which seemed to be the bird's intention. He watched the bird through one open eye, annoyed at this very noisy little fellow. He opened the other eye to look around for something to throw at the aggravating little creature. Before he could locate anything suitable, the bird, spoke to him, "Lay still! Lay still!" commanded Yellow Throat. Sitting Bull was frightened. He had never before been spoken to by a bird, although he knew that all creatures can talk to the Lakota when and if, they wished.

"Lay still! Lay still!" Yellow Throat said again.

Then, from the corner of Sitting Bull's eye, he saw Grizzly. He lay very, very still, as though he were dead. Bear was now upon him. It reared up on its hind legs and roared. It was huge. Sitting Bull still played Possum. Bear dropped back to its normal walking position and gave Sitting Bull a prod.

Sitting Bull still did not dare move. Bear's hair was brushing his skin and it tickled; but he knew if he moved, Bear would certainly kill him.

Sitting Bull took a very shallow breath through his nose trying not to move at all. The smell of Bear's rancid breath was about to choke him, but still he was motionless. The bird twittered and scolded Bear from the nearby tree branch. It seemed to distract Bear. Thinking Sitting Bull was dead, Bear gave him one last prod. Bored with Sitting Bull's lack of movement, Grizzly Bear turned his attentions to the noisy bird. It roared its disapproval at the Yellow Throat, then lumbered slowly off to find something more interesting to lavish its attentions on.

When Sitting Bull could no longer hear Bear, he opened his eyes to see it disappearing into the bushes on the far side of the clearing. He got up, still very frightened. The bird was still watching from its perch, now quiet. Realizing the bird had saved his life, Sitting Bull raised his hands in the gesture of blessing and addressed Yellow Throat:

"Pretty bird, you saw me and took pity on me; you wish me to survive among my People. This day, you have saved my life. Oh, Bird People, from this day always you shall be my relatives."

Another bird—a Meadow Lark—would speak to Sitting Bull on another occasion. Alas that would be a very sad occasion, for it would foretell of Sitting Bull's demise at the hands of his own People.

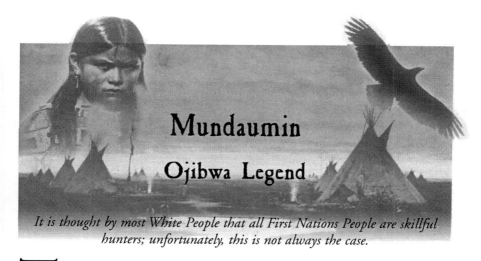

Mundaumin

Ojibwa Legend

It is thought by most White People that all First Nations People are skillful hunters; unfortunately, this is not always the case.

There lived a family whose father was not an accomplished hunter, and his wife and children often went hungry. One thing they had plenty of was love, and for that, they thanked Great Spirit. The eldest of the children in the family was a boy called Wunzh. He was a good, obedient boy of generous, honorable character. But as much as he tried, like his father, he was far from a great hunter.

One morning in the Spring, his father came to Wunzh and said, "You are of age to seek your Vision, my son, to find the Spirit that will guide you through your adult life."

The very next day, his father took Wunzh out to a lonely spot in the forest where he had chosen a location for the Sweat Lodge they would build.

They cut Willow saplings to be the frame for the lodge and dug a pit to hold the red hot stones that would be wetted down to make steam. They then covered the structure with hides they had brought.

Wunzh's father took his Pipe from its Pouch and filled it with Sacred Herbs and Tobacco. He then lit the Pipe and Prayed to the Four Directions and asked Creator to bless the Sweat Lodge. They also asked Mother Earth for forgiveness for the killing of the Willow and the animals that had given their hides for the Sweat lodge covering. He then also Prayed that the young boy's Quest would be successful.

Using the Sweat Lodge they had completed would cleanse the young man's body. Huddling in the dark alone amidst the purifying steam, he would clear his mind so the Spirits could communicate with him. His abstinence from food would last five Suns and then his father would return to the Quest Site with nourishment.

During the first two days of his fast, Wunzh wandered through the forest. He was very interested in plants and tried to identify all that he saw. His father had taught him many things about the vegetation which inhabited the forest and he tried to remember the medicinal uses they possessed. Wunzh found some foliage he had not seen before and he vowed to experiment with it, to find out what uses it might have after his Quest was finished. Sometimes, he would sit quietly and watch the birds and animals go about their business, learning from them all the time.

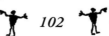

On the third morning Wunzh awoke and did not have the strength to go for another walk. He lay quietly alone in his lodge, still fasting and waiting patiently for the Spirits to come. Wunzh closed his eyes tightly and Prayed to Creator, "Great Spirit, to You we owe everything. I humbly ask You to make it easier for my People to feed themselves. Some of our People are great hunters and they and their families and friends eat well. Others, like my father, and, for that matter, me, are not good at hunting. Sometimes our family goes hungry. I ask for a Vision that will help the Honorable and respectful hunters like my father who do not have the skills to provide their families with food."

With the Prayer finished, Wunzh opened his eyes. Standing before him was a handsome, beautifully dressed Man. His robes were as green as the leaves in the forest. In His jet black hair, He wore brown, feathery plumes.

"I am Mundaumin," He said. "I have been sent to you by Great Spirit who made all things on Earth and in the Heavens. You are a very unselfish boy. You have not asked for the gift of the warrior or for wealth, but to help your father and your Tribe. I will instruct you in how this will be achieved. You must wrestle Me, that is the way I will know if you are sincere with your wish."

Wunzh was very weak from fasting, but the words of the Spirit brought strength to his heart as he stood and prepared to wrestle. They wrestled for quite some time. Just as Wunzh was about to give up through sheer exhaustion, the Spirit said, "That is enough for now. I will return to try you again tomorrow." Mundaumin ascended into the Sky.

Wunzh slept soundly that night, even though he was very hungry. The wrestling had all but worn him out.

The next afternoon, the Spirit returned. "I am here to test you again, Wunzh. You must wrestle Me," He said.

Wunzh was so tired he could hardly stand, but he decided it would be better to die than to fail in his Vision Quest. So, he stood trembling before the Spirit and they began to wrestle. Wunzh could feel the Spirit was not using all the strength he could bring to bear on him. He was thankful for that. Soon, as before, the Spirit stopped the contest and said, "Wunzh, I will return one more time. But, tomorrow, you must beat Me. Only then can I grant what you seek." Once again, the Spirit lifted into the Sky.

That night, Wunzh dared not move. He slept as much as he possibly could, trying to conserve what little strength he had. He decided that he would win this final wrestling match or die trying.

The next afternoon, the Spirit arrived and said, "Are you ready for the decisive match, Wunzh? Remember, you must beat Me." Wunzh staggered to his feet and nodded he was ready.

The two struggled with each other. Wunzh focused his mind on one throw, one that would use all the strength he had left in his body. When he felt the opportunity was there, Wunzh used every drop of energy he could muster and slammed his opponent to the ground.

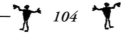

"I am defeated," said the Spirit. "Your Quest is won. Your wish for your People will be granted. Now, sit, and I will give you final instructions." The Spirit continued, saying, "Tomorrow morning is the sixth day of your Quest. Your father will come to you with food. You must refuse it. You must fast for one more day until Sundown tomorrow. During this time, you must prepare a plot of ground. This ground must be in a clearing that receives good Sunlight. You must dig the plot over and make it soft. Take all the plants from it. The Earth must be clean of all vegetation. After Father Sun has reached the center of the Sky, I will come to you. You will throw me down for the last time and I will die."

"No, Spirit, you must not die for me," said the astonished boy.

"Listen, Wunzh, don't talk," admonished the Spirit. "You will take my outer robes from my body and bury me in the soft ground that you have prepared. You will leave me there. Wunzh, you know most of the plants of this land. You must keep my grave free from plants and roots. When you see ones sprouting on my grave that you have never seen before, leave them. These plants will be Great Spirit's gift to the Ojibwa. These plants will have big seed pods that look like ears. Inside the robes of the ears, you will find the seeds. As your Quest requested, these seeds will sustain the unsuccessful hunters and their families."

Wunzh watched the Spirit disappear for the last time. The next morning, just as the Spirit had foretold, Wunzh's father appeared with a bowl of meat for his son.

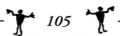

"Father, I must not eat. I have been visited by a Spirit and my Quest is nearly over. I will be home this evening. I will eat then."

Wunzh's father was very happy that his son's Quest appeared to be going well.

Early in the afternoon, the Spirit returned for the final time. "Well, Wunzh, are you ready to throw me to the ground?"

Wunzh summoned the last of his strength and hurled the Spirit to the ground. The Spirit lay there, motionless. He was dead. As directed, Wunzh removed the Spirit's green robes and the brown, feathery headdress, leaving the Spirit clothed only in his bright yellow breach-cloth. Wunzh dug a deep hole, then pulled the body of the Spirit to it, lowered it in and covered it up. The task done, Wunzh sadly left to rejoin his family.

He never spoke of his Vision Quest, knowing that it was not over. Every few days, he would go and remove any recognizable vegetation from the Spirit's grave and say a Prayer for the Spirit.

One day Wunzh was cleaning the Spirit's grave when he noticed strange shoots, shoots of a kind he had never seen before.

"These must be the plants that the Spirit, Mundaumin, spoke of," Wunzh thought. He cleared the plot of all but the new shoots. He then carefully dug around them to loosen the Earth, so moisture could get to the roots. He kept up his vigil until the Summer was almost gone, cleaning the

Earth and caring for the plants. When the nights began to turn cooler, he knew it was time to tell his father.

Wunzh and his father arrived at the grave site and Wunzh showed his father the beautiful, tall, plants waving in the light breeze.

"Father, this was the Spirit's gift to our People," Wunzh said. His father didn't understand. "Father, you see the ears that grow from the sides of the plant? They contain seeds that we can eat. These strange plants greatly resemble the Spirit that came to me. They have the color of his robes and his brown, feathery headdress." Wunzh peeled back the outer layer of one of the ears a little, revealing the bright yellow seeds. "Look, this was the color of his breach-cloth. Father, in my Quest, I asked the Great Spirit to give the Ojibwa food they would not have to kill for. When I defeated Mundaumin in a wrestling match, He told me the Ojibwa would eat of His flesh. This is what He gave us."

Wunzh and his father gathered some of the ears and took them back to the village. They peeled the robes back from the ears before feasting, leaving the bright yellow kernels clinging to the husks. Some, they ate raw, others they put into boiling water. They roasted the rest over the fire. They all agreed, it was delicious.

The great gift from the Spirit Mundaumin was Maize (Corn).

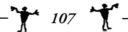

Loneliness

Cree Legend

Grief is a painful emotion, but through its healing power (and the sage counsel of Loon), one young man learns to release the past and live again.

The young man's condition had worsened drastically in the past few days. Since the passing of his wife to the Spirit World, it was as though he had nothing left to live for and now was willing himself to die. His eyesight had started to fail and he coughed incessantly. He was gravely ill. It was thought by the Elders that with Winter coming, the young man would not live to see another Earth Renewal—Spring.

He sat alone in his lodge, grieving. "If only we could have been blessed with children, then I would have someone to share my sorrow," he thought selfishly. In one hand, he grasped tightly a pure white, bone necklace and remembered his wife fondly.

The loving couple had been at their favorite spot, a beautiful lake not far from their village. They had both stripped and bathed. They swam together, frolicking and splashing each other like happy children. When they finally left the water, they made love, wonderful passionate love. It was a beautiful time. He had given her the necklace as a present, a surprise. He had made the necklace himself and it had taken many Round Moons to complete it. It was a work of great love. She loved it and the necklace became her pride and joy. She made a huge fuss over the gift.

"It will always remind me of this day, and our love for each other," she had said. Then they kissed, deep and long. A smile came to his lips in reverie.

"That's it," he thought. "The lake—that's where I will go. I will end my life at our lake. It will be a fitting place to rejoin my beautiful wife."

He set off immediately. The young man had walked that trail many times with his wife which was just as well because his eyesight was of little help to him. He fell many times. But his determination drove him onward. Eventually he reached his destination—the beautiful lake. He sat on a rock all alone staring out at the water, but not seeing anything of its beauty. He still held his wife's favorite possession, the white bone necklace.

A strange sound came to him. It was the lonely cry of Loon. Loon cried again. It was as though Loon were talking to him.

"What do you want, Loon? Are you talking to me?"

"Yes, I am talking to you," said Loon. "I recognize you. Where is your pretty wife? Why are you so unhappy? "

The young man told Loon about her passing. Loon commiserated, telling him how sorry he was. Then Loon said in a very affirming way, "It is time for you to rejoin the living. You are young. You will have many more Winters among your People."

"Loon, I do not wish to live anymore. I wish to be with my beautiful wife," replied the young man. "Anyway, I am very ill. Even my sight has all but left me. I am about to die."

"No. You will be with your wife soon enough. You are lonely and you feel sorry for yourself. That is not an excuse for death. Grab my tail. Come with me. I will guide you," demanded Loon.

The young man did not really want to go with Loon. But he did as he was told. Loon led the man into the lake. Soon they were swimming out into the deeper water.

"I am too weak to go further," gasped the young man.

"Hold on tight," ordered Loon. With that, Loon dove deeply, dragging the young man with him under the cold water.

The young man thought he would surely die, right there and then, and wondered if Loon was trying to drown him. But it was not the case. Loon suddenly turned and started up toward the light. With the young man's, lungs bursting, they broke the surface.

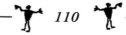

A strange thing had happened. The young man could see. His eyesight had been restored. He looked at Loon and asked, ""How can this be, Loon? I was all but blind."

"You are far too young to die, so I have given you your eyesight and strength back. Now, let go of my tail. We will swim back to shore."

This they did. The young man felt healthier than he ever had. But still, he felt lonely and grieved for his dead wife.

Loon sensed this and said, "You must let her go, young man. She has passed on and I'm sure she is happy. She is with our Creator in the Spirit World. You to must learn how to be happy again. Only think about the good thing that happened to you both. You must realize that many People are never given what you two had. Let your sad memories go. Be thankful for that gift of true love."

The young man thought about Loon's words, then hung his head in shame. "You are right, Loon, I will go back to the village, I will carry on. But, I will always remember her," he said.

"Of course, that is how it should be. But, as I have said, remember the good," advised Loon. "Be happy, not sad."

The young man still clasped the white bone necklace in his hand. A thought came to him. "This choker was my beautiful bride's favorite thing," he said. "In fact, I gave it to her at the edge of this very lake." He leaned forward, thrusting the necklace toward Loon. "Now I wish you to have it."

Loon hesitated. The very thought of being given such a treasure affected him deeply. He thought for a moment, then said, "I will be proud to wear such a wonderful, symbol of love."

And so it was. The necklace was given to proud Loon. From that day, he has worn it with great dignity. Every now and then, he will sadly call his lonely cry, remembering the young man's devotion to his beautiful wife.

Why Moose Has Loose Skin

OjiCree Legend

It's said that clothes make the man, but among the animals, Wisakachak's tailoring is as much about warmth as it is about style.

Long ago, before People came to this land, the animals and birds were here. The birds had feathers of different colors; but, in those days, the animals were all the same color, sort of a pink-gray. None had the beautiful fur they now have. All of the animals and birds lived together in one big happy family. There was no fighting because none was conceited about his appearance. Everyone was friendly, Muskwa (Bear) with Waboose (Rabbit), Pisseu (Lynx) with Sakwaseu (Mink). Even Maheengun (Wolf) was on speaking terms with all the other animals.

Then came a very cold Winter, one colder than anyone could ever remember. All the animals suffered greatly, some even got severely frost bitten. They had to huddle together to keep warm.

Finally Spring arrived. The soft Southern Winds gently warmed the land, fattening the buds on the trees, bringing forth the songs from the Frogs and nesting birds.

Muskwa called a Council. "This Winter was so cold that some of our People could have died," he said. "We must get Wisakachak to ask Gitchi Manitou (Great Spirit) for some protection against such frigid cold."

"Good idea," said Waboose. "Let's ask for something warm to wear in the Winter, but something we can shed in the Summer."

And so it was that the animals took their idea to Wisakachak who promised to pass it on to Great Spirit.

Creator had seen the animal's plight through the harsh Winter and was only too pleased to grant them some protection. He set Wisakachak the task of making Winter coats for all the animals in a variety of styles and colors. All Summer, Wisakachak worked feverishly, getting all the coats ready. Finally, in the Moon of Golden Leaves, just before Wey Wey(Geese) head South for the Winter, all was ready.

Wisakachak sent Chipmunk (Zhaashaagowaabik) to tell all the animals their Winter coats were ready and to come to His cave right away to pick out the coats they wanted. First come, first served was the order of the day.

All the animals rushed off to Wisakachak's cave to get their new coats, all save greedy Mooswa (Moose). He stayed in the middle of the river practicing his favorite pastime, eating. Mooswa loved to eat, especially those succulent plants and shoots that grew below the river's surface. Mooswa would look up lazily from his underwater grazing from time to time, noticing the animals as they came from Wisakachak's cave with their fine new coats. Some came right down to the water's edge, to admire their new furs in the river's reflection.

Mooswa, finally full with food, decided he would go and get his new coat. He lumbered off to Wisakachak's cave. When he got there, there was only one robe left, a great big one, too big for even Mooswa. As it was the only one left and he knew Winter was coming, Mooswa put the bulky coat on and wandered back to the river. He was hungry again. Mooswa didn't seem at all concerned that his coat didn't fit very well. He never even asked Wisakachak to alter it. Which is why, when you see Moose, he looks like he's wearing his big brother's clothes.

After the animals got their new coats, a lot of them got very conceited about their appearance and stopped talking to each other. Some still don't speak to one another. But those who did still communicate and all agree Mooswa looks funny in his coat.

Why Butterflies Flutter

Ute Legend

Tricking the Trickster takes exceptional talent and not a small amount of teamwork.

Coyote was doing what Coyote does best—sleeping.

Coyote's wife was fed up with His inert lifestyle and decided it was time He did some real work. She shook Him quite vigorously to awaken Him. His eyes opened slowly and Coyote gave His wife a long hard stare. His wife asked her sleepy husband. No. She demanded that He fetch salt from the Great Salt Lake for cooking.

"Now," she shouted at her sleepy husband.

"The Great Salt Lake is so far away," He whined. A stony stare from His wife was all He needed to convince Himself that He'd better get on with the task.

So He arose and immediately, but reluctantly, set off. He wondered to Himself why He had to do all the hard things in life. It was such a long journey over the Uinta Mountains and down to the valley below where the Great Salt Lake was. By the time Coyote got to His destination, He was completely exhausted. Coyote sat and thought about the daunting job ahead—the collection of salt.

Something strange flitted around Him. Suddenly, the air was filled with color, Dancing Flowers—Butterflies. They also had come to the lake for life-giving salt. They were there in great numbers. The colors of the fluttering insects mesmerized Coyote. His eyelids were getting heavier and heavier. Soon He fell into His favorite pastime—sleep.

Monarch, the Leader of the Butterflies, flew up to the sleeping canine to take a closer look. He recognized the famous Trickster right away.

"Let's play a trick on Coyote," he whispered to the other Butterflies. "Come over here, quick, come here." They all congregated over the slumbering Coyote. They decided they would lift the sleeping Trickster without waking him and take Him back to where He lived.

Each of the Butterflies took hold of one single Coyote hair and with one coordinated effort, they gently lifted Coyote into the air. Then they carried Him back over the Uinta Mountains, back to His lodge. After gently placing Him in his favorite sleeping area, they left quickly.

Coyote's wife was away hunting when the Butterflies arrived. You can imagine she was quite distraught when she found her sleeping husband and thought He had not yet set off to get the salt.

She wakened Him again, this time by shouting loudly into His pointed ears. Some of the things she shouted I would never write down. They were far too rude. Coyote jumped from His bed, totally confused. He could not understand. He was sure He had arrived at the lake. "I suppose it must have been a dream," He said, shaking His head in disbelief. "But, if it was a dream, then why am I so tired? I will set off immediately, My Wife. I do not understand what happened here."

"Why are You so tired? Laziness happened, Coyote. Laziness. The very thought of work makes You tired," She snapped.

Off Coyote loped, wondering why He had married such a grumpy female. As you can imagine, He was completely worn out when He reached the Great Salt Lake for the second time. This time He knew He could not snooze until the job was done, so He took His sack and started to collect the precious salt, not stopping until the sack was full. Once the job was completed, He lay down to take a well-earned nap.

Again Monarch, Leader of the Dancing Flowers—the Butterflies, decided to play the same trick on the Trickster, as it had worked so well before. The Butterflies once more picked up the sleeping Coyote. This time, they also picked up His sack of salt and carried both over the Uinta Mountains to His lodge. As the Dancing Flowers entered the lodge, they met Coyote's wife. Monarch, the Leader of the Butterflies, explained what had happened both times, whispering so as not to awaken the famous Trickster. She laughed and promised not to tell her conceited Husband the truth.

"At last," she confided. "I know something that my dear Husband does not. Don't worry, My beautiful friends, your secret is safe with me. Very safe."

To this day, Coyote does not know the truth. He tells of His strange dream to anyone who will listen. Believe me, there aren't many who will. Of course, the dream He relates is the one where He went to the Salt Lake twice. Even coming home with salt the second time, but never leaving his lodge....

The story has great importance among the Butterfly Tribe, as well. Once one pupates from the chrysalis to an adult Butterfly, it is told the story of Coyote being tricked by the Dancing Flowers. And this is why Butterflies appear to have no predetermined flight plan.

The reason they cannot fly straight is they are all very amused by the tale, and they're still laughing at the grand joke they played on the Trickster Coyote. So willy-nilly, they wander the World, crashing into the odd object, fluttering up and down, back and forth, always giggling, just tickled pink or red or blue!

It is said if you whisper your secrets to the Dancing Flowers, they will take them to Creator. The Southern Native Americans also have great respect for Butterflies, going as far as to call their eggs Seeds of Happiness, which I believe they truly are.

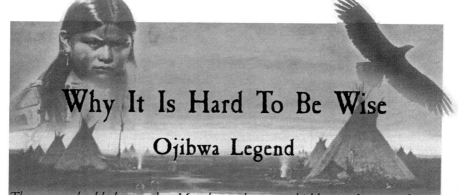

Why It Is Hard To Be Wise

Ojibwa Legend

The most valuable lessons that Man has to learn are hidden in the most obvious and also the most difficult-to-find place.

Before the Two-Leggeds came, Creator went among those who already existed on Earth Mother to explain His intentions.

"Gather around Me, all you Fish People, all you Wing Flappers and all you Four-Leggeds. I have something of great importance to tell you."

They all did as Creator asked. He then continued, "I have decided to put a new being among you, a Two-Legged. This being will be capable of causing you all much harm. But this creature will also have compassion, humor, honesty and a good understanding of the Sacred Circle and Earth Mother. There are two special things that I wish to give the Two-Leggeds, but I do not want to make it easy for them to find them. In fact, they must be very difficult to locate. These new beings will have to find these things before they can use them; but with these gifts, the Two-Leggeds will become whole. The two things I speak of are Wisdom and Justice. These are the things they will need to exist in harmony with all of you and with each other. Where shall I hide these things? Help Me, My Children."

Buffalo lumbered forward and said, "I will hide these Sacred things, Creator. Put them on my hump. I will carry them to the Prairies where my People reign. These Two-Leggeds will not find them easily there."

To which Creator responded by saying, "Unfortunately, Buffalo, you and the Two-Leggeds will soon be one. There will be many of them living with you on the vast grasslands. They will revere you, but you will not necessarily respect them. On the prairies, Wisdom and Justice would be too easily found."

Creator then asked, "Are there any other suggestions?"

"Yes," said Salmon. "I will take Wisdom and Justice to the head waters of the rivers where I lay my eggs. I will bury them there."

"Oh, Salmon. I wish it would be as easy as that," said Creator. "I fear the Two-Leggeds would find them right away. Just as Bear has already found you, so will the Two-Leggeds."

All the Peoples who were gathered were mystified at the problem. Most just shook their heads, very confused about these Two-Leggeds.

Then Bear stepped forward and said, "Give these things to me, Creator. I will take them to the falls where I fish for my life-giver, Salmon. I will hide these things under the water where the falls are. The Two-Leggeds will not find them there."

Creator said to Bear, "He will easily find Wisdom and Justice there, Bear. Just as I have already told Salmon, he will also find you."

"He will be sorry if he finds me. I will chase him away. I may even destroy him, I will guard Wisdom and Justice with my life," roared Bear.

Creator said in answer to Bear's emotional outburst, "He will not fear you. His cunning will be a good match for your mighty strength."

Eagle came forward and said, "Creator, I will take these Sacred things to the highest mountains, to the places where only I can go. I will hide them there."

"These Two-Leggeds will climb your mountains just for fun, Eagle. I am afraid they will find Wisdom and Justice too easily there."

Creator then continued with a very worried look on His face, "Does anyone else have the solution?"

No one offered a response for a long time. Suddenly, tiny Mole scuttled forward and said in a soft, squeaky voice, "Creator, if You wish these Two-Leggeds to have great difficulty in finding these virtues, why don't You hide them in the Seventh Direction. Hide the virtues, Wisdom and Justice, inside these Two-Legged creatures. Let them learn to seek within themselves. For, as we know, to look inward is one of the hardest things to do. It sounds to me as if these Two-Leggeds will lack the perception to do this."

Creator smiled and said, "Mole, you are one of My smallest Creations and one of the very wisest. That is where I will put Wisdom and Justice. Only the most perceptive of the Two-Leggeds will be able to discover these wonderful gifts."

Oshkitaapahk

Ojibwa Legend

I t is hard to believe, but there was a time when there was no such thing as War, no hostility of any kind. Right here on Mother Earth, all the People and animals got along exceptionally well. There was always plenty to eat, and there weren't even any really cold days—no Winter. Earth was a much more beautiful place than it is today.

On Earth, the People laughed and enjoyed each other's company, cherishing every waking moment. Their time was taken up with all sorts of games and pleasant activities. The children never, ever shed a tear of fear or hunger; no-one abused anyone. Life on Earth was wonderful.

At night, the Star People—whose worlds were not nearly as peaceful as Earth's—would watch the Earth People with envy. As they looked down from the Heavens at the Earth's idyllic situation below, they yearned for something similar in their Worlds. The Earth People would just sit and watch the Stars out of curiosity.

This story is about one Anishnabe—Ojibwa, village and its inhabitants. The village lay nestled by a lake and was surrounded on three sides by Fir and Birch trees. It was a beautiful place to live.

One night, while the villagers sat watching the Skies, they noticed that one of the Stars seemed particularly radiant, more glowing than it had ever appeared before. Its position seemed closer to their village than usual.

The next night, the Star was even brighter. It seemed to be getting closer and closer to the village, now appearing to be just above the hills in the adjoining valley, about a day's walk away. The People decided that, if the Star was any nearer the next night, they would send a party to visit it.

That night, one of the young men from the village had an unusual Dream. In his Dream a Beautiful Woman came to him. She was dressed in pure white, flowing robes and Her hair seemed to be spun from gold.

"I am the Spirit of the Star that sits above your village," She said." I came to your land to live with you, to be as you are. I want to be close to the happiness that is generated by you good and kind People; but alas, My body is not suited to life here and I can only visit you in Dreams. I cannot exist on Earth as you do, but, I do not want to return to My own Land, I am so happy here. If I stay, I will die. Can you please help Me find a way to remain in this wonderful place?" With that said, the Star smiled in a sad sort of way. The young man's Dream then faded.

The next morning, the young man told his People of the Star's Dream Visit and of Her plight. There was a lot of discussion among the Elders during the day about ways to help the Star. It was decided that the best thing to do would be to commune with Creator for guidance, asking help for the Star Maiden.

That evening, all the People came out to see the radiant Star that now hovered above the lake. They prayed to Creator for permission for the Star to remain with them on Earth. The Star heard their prayers and was deeply moved by the generosity of the People But, She knew She would have to return to Her Star World, or die.

Suddenly, without any warning, She exploded in a mass of shimmering lights that shot from Her once beautiful body, rending Her into a million pieces. Her broken, fragmented body fell, seemingly insignificantly, into the lake below. Her longing for what She could not attain had broken Her heart.

The People, for the first time in their lives, felt genuine sadness. They all prayed that the Star's Spirit be blessed.

Early next morning, at first light, the young man who had spoken to the Star in his Dream arose did his Sunrise Ceremony and went down to the lake to bathe. There, to his amazement, was something he had never witnessed before. Lying on the surface of the water, there was a myriad of snow white blossoms with bright golden centers sitting on pads of light green. Thousands of these spectacular flowers dotted the lake.

Creator had given the Star Woman Her wish. Even though Her body had been shattered, She had been granted Her dream—to stay with the Earth People forever. Every Summer since then, She has been able to watch the People, especially the children, She loved to watch them play and be close to them—for, from each tiny, broken piece of Her body that landed in the lake, a beautiful flower, a pure white Water Lily—Oshkitaapahk had grown.

When you arise in the morning,
give thanks for the morning light,
for your life and strength.
Give thanks for your food
and the joy of living.
If you see no reason for
giving thanks, the fault
lies within yourself.

Tecumseh
Shawnee Chief